COOKING

CHILLIES

Recipes and Ideas to Make
the Most of a Chilli Harvest

JASON NICKELS

Cooking Chillies

Recipes and Ideas to Make the Most of a Chilli Harvest

Author: Jason Nickels

Published by: Jason Nickels

ISBN: 978-0-9574446-4-5

First Edition, 2014

Published in the United Kingdom

Designed by Chandler Book Design
www.chandlerbookdesign.co.uk

TABLE OF CONTENTS

Introduction

Introduction

Chilli growing can be a terrible trap to fall into, you may start with a small plant, a gift or an impulse purchase; you might care for it, neglect it, give it a name, or not, but when the first chilli appears you fall in love with it, and when the time comes to cook it, you chop it with reverence.

This is how most chilli growers begin, and of all those legions of people who now have chilli plants crammed into every window, every corner of their greenhouse, most of them started this way; their addiction never quite satisfied. Others start with heat, they like spicy food and the effect it has; they crave more, try different flavours, different chillies, hotter ones, and then hotter still. These two tribes, the grower and the eater, meet in the middle, and they overlap, and the result is a craving for all things chilli. Grow them, cook them, dry them, pickle them, eat them, make them saucy and make them sweet. This book is for all of those people, something to help you make the most of your journey of chilli discovery.

In 2003, when I started out in commercial chilli farming, making sauces and all that goes with it, chillies were a fledgling industry in the UK. In those days many of the ingredients used in this book weren't widely available, and if you wanted to grow chillies yourself just finding seeds was difficult. These were the days when cookery books asked for just red chilli, green chilli, or chilli powder, but nothing more specific, and you could count the number of specialist chilli suppliers on one hand. If you did get your hands on a chilli cook book from the USA, and the chances are it would have been Mark Miller's *Great Chile Book*, you could have been left frustrated because the crucial ingredients weren't easily available. Roll on 12 years, and we now have a thriving and diverse chilli industry in the UK. There are hundreds of companies growing, cooking and importing, so that often the things you need to make your recipes the way you want them are only as far away as your nearest farmers' market, supermarket, or, at worse, a day away on the internet. The catch-22 of cookery books dumbing down their recipes to suit the ingredients available to their readers, and readers frustrated that they can't get the ingredients for authentic recipes are over; so I have every faith in the fact that none of the recipes in this book will frustrate you. I hope the tips, tricks and recipes help you make the most your chilli crop or your overflowing larder and all I ask is that if you only ever make one recipe from this book, make the last one, ginger chillentines.

The Global Spread of the Chilli, and its Uses in Different Cultures

Chillies have been used in cooking since pre-history, evidence of their use has been found around old fireplaces from 4 thousand years ago. So modern man doesn't have a monopoly on the love-hate relationship we enjoy with the heat of the chilli.

Before selective breeding began, the chillies used in cooking would have been picked from the wild, or cultivated from wild seed. These ancestors of modern chillies were inevitably small, hot, red chillies. Once humans settled into pastoral farming rather than nomadic lifestyles then the process of breeding from the best and tastiest plants would have meant that chillies started to evolve from their wild ancestors into something closer to the diverse range we enjoy today.

This all took place in South and Central America, and it wasn't until the Portuguese and Spanish started invading these areas that trading started and chillies were exported to their other colonies, eventually finding their way to just about every warm or tropical corner of the globe. Nowadays chillies are not only diverse in their range of different varieties, but in their geographical spread too, with a more cosmopolitan coverage than wheat, potatoes, rice, and just about anything else.

The Scoville Heat Scale and the Chilli Burn

Traditionally, the heat of chillies is conveyed in Scoville units. Named after a scientist in 1912, the Scoville scale was a simple dilution test conducted using a willing panel of tasters who decided whether or not the heat could be detected in a diluted, sugary chilli solution. The experiment was simple, if a little arbitrary. If he could dilute something 100,000 times and the chilli was just detectable, then this would represent 100,000 Scoville Heat Units (SHU). Nowadays there is a more accurate way of measurement, using liquid chromatography to detect the level of capsaicin (the chemical that generates the sensation of heat). This is translated into Scoville Units, 1 part-per million of capsaicin being 15 SHU, which means neat, chemically extracted, capsaicin will be around 15 million SHU.

Even given this level of accurate chemical analysis, results can be unhelpful. Test results from different laboratories can vary greatly. Capsaicin isn't just one chemical, there are a range of similar capsaicin chemicals, some or all of which may be present at different levels in a chilli. A chilli picked from the first node of a plant, grown in full sun, will measure hotter than one picked from a shady branch. All this means that results are often 'hotly' disputed. Some people will tell you that certain types of chilli will 'feel' hotter than they actually are, so take the figures in this book, or anywhere else, as guidelines; be prepared to formulate your own arguments and join in the debate with an eye to friendly rivalry and good humour.

Fresh Chillies, Dried Chillies and the Best Ones to Choose

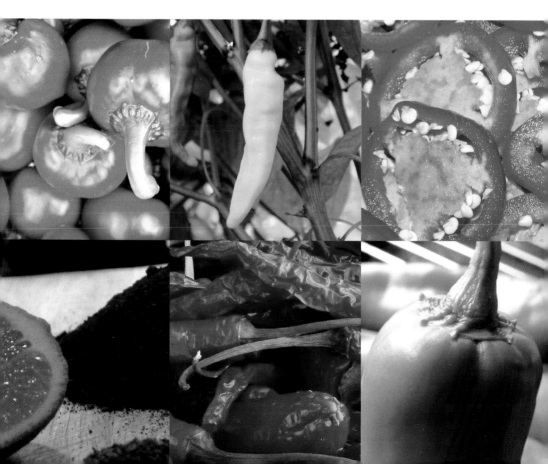

CHAPTER 1

Fresh Chillies, Dried Chillies and the Best Ones to Choose

Of the many varieties of chilli available to buy, be it fresh, dried or smoked, there is a fairly short list with which you can achieve most things. Some chillies are grown specifically to be dried, some don't dry very well, and some are good for both and even take on a different name when they are dried. I'd love for every chilli to be available to all of us at all times, unfortunately this isn't the case, but if you can get your hands on most of the list below, either by buying them or growing them yourself, then you will have enough of an arsenal to cover just about any chilli recipe you come across.

Aji

The South American aji chillies, of which there are hundreds, provide a distinctive sharp and citrusy heat, quite distinctive and very useful to the cook, especially when it comes to fish, or providing an additional note to sweet dishes where it can provide a sharp zing. They are frequently dried, most of them dry very easily and, although the flavour changes slightly, they are still used for the same purposes as the fresh ones. They are rewarding to grow as they are quite tough and resilient, but tend to grow on quite large plants so you will need plenty of space.

Ali Limon

Aji Limo / Limon / Lemon Drop

This is a hot version, around 50,000 SHU; easy to grow and dry yourself, and can be bought fresh from specialist growers.

Aji Amarillo

This is the more popular variety and used in lots of Peruvian cooking. It is milder, around 3,000 SHU, and therefore often used in quite large quantities, again for its sharper zesty flavour.

Aji Amarillo

Ancho / Poblano / Mulato

The poblano chilli is a large fruit, shaped like an elongated heart, from 13-20 cm long, and 8 cm wide at the top. It has a mild heat, maybe 2,000 SHU. When fresh and green it is cherished for its firm, tasty flesh and is either stuffed, or cut into strips; there are recipes for both later in this book. The flavour and texture is something unique, so for this reason it is worth trying to grow them yourself if you can.

Ancho comes from a type which ripens to red and ancho mulato from a type which ripens to dark brown.

Apart from basic red chilli powder I would say the ancho is one of the most useful and versatile dried chilli available. It adds an additional depth of flavour, one of sweet dried fruit. The mulato flavour is less sweet and more intense, more like liquorice and tobacco.

When left to ripen to its final colour, and then dried, the poblano becomes known either as ancho, or ancho mulato.

Apache

'Apache' has a place in my heart as it is often the plant on which a new chilli grower cuts their teeth. They are compact, probably the quickest chilli to ripen, which makes them great for beginners, and because they are often available to buy as fruiting plants, they are an impulse purchase. So they do their job in providing hundreds of small, fairly hot and tasty chillies, thereby securing their owner's addiction to chilli growing for ever more. If you only ever grow one chilli plant, don't have much space and just want a regular supply of small, hot red chillies, then 'Apache' is for you. They also dry very easily so you can make your own hot red powder with them.

Cayenne

Generally, cooks recognise cayenne as a type of chilli powder, often referred to as hot, but in comparison to chillies generally, it isn't that spicy at all. Cayenne is a city in French Guyana, on the north coast of South America, so it is likely that the name originates from the spice that French traders brought to Europe. Nowadays the name has stuck to any type of *Capsicum annuum* chilli that is long, thin, thin-fleshed and easily dried, be they hot or mild. Examples from other parts of the world are long slim cayenne, khung pao, 'Joe's Long' or 'Ring of Fire'. Whilst they can be used fresh, they are quite tough, and apart from a bit of heat don't add much, so they are generally used in the powdered form where they will give a good red colour as well as a bit of heat.

Cherry and Cilegia Chillies

Small, cherry-like chillies pickled in a jar are a popular appetiser, either on their own or stuffed with feta cheese. There are numerous varieties that will fit the bill as being suitable for this purpose, from cillegia piccante for a bumper crop of smaller ones, to 'Cherry Bomb', which are larger and better for stuffing. The key to making your favourite pickle is more about how you treat them than the chilli you start out with. There is a recipe for this later in the book. If you haven't used them fresh and don't want to pickle them you can dry them fairly easily, and obviously freeze them too.

Chipotle

Strictly speaking this isn't a variety of chilli, it is a word used to describe smoked chillies of many different types. Chipotle (pronounced chipotlay), is a Nahuatl (an old Mexican language) word for smoked chilli. It could mean any type of chilli, but most commonly it will be a jalapeño.

Wherever you see the word chipotle listed as an ingredient or hear the word on its own, the chances are it is a type called morita to which they refer, these are smoked and dried red jalapeños. Other smoked chillies such as meco or ahumado are made with different chillies or smoked in a different way. Morita are 3 cm long, wrinkled, dark brown or almost black and with a strong smoky flavour and commonly used as a flavouring in anything from crisps to mayonnaise. I always keep them in stock either whole, as powder, or both. They are a versatile ingredient I couldn't survive without. One of the pleasures of growing your own chillies is that it gives you plenty of scope for smoking them yourself, a process described later in this book, and something that I would recommend you try.

Espelette (Pimente d'Espelette)

The town of Espelette lies in the Basque region of South West France, and the chilli of the same name enjoys *Appellation d'Origine Contrôlée* which means that peppers sold under the Espelette name can only be grown in that region. This makes them difficult to get hold of and therefore something that you may benefit from growing yourself. If you can dry enough of them they will last for a long time hanging on a string in your kitchen. It is a thin fleshed, slightly spicy, paprika-type chilli, which lends itself well to drying and is usually used in flavouring cured meat, where it imparts a deep red colour, and as a general seasoning in Basque cookery.

© Electrowan / Dreamstime.com

Guajillo

Guajillo is a useful Mexican variety, tougher and thicker skinned, about 10-12 cm long, slightly hotter than the bigger New Mexico chillies, around 3,000-5,000 SHU, and a dark red colour. It can be used dried or powdered and is very useful if your needs are for something slightly hotter than mild or hot New Mexico powder.

Habaneros or Scotch Bonnets

For me, along with the majority of regular chilli cooks, these are probably used more frequently than any other, though usually in quite small quantities. These are the ones used in Caribbean cookery and also lend themselves to spicy desserts because of their fruity fragrance. A little goes a long way and many of the recipes in this book call for just a half or a quarter of a whole one. The easiest way of preserving these, whether they are home-grown or from a shop, is to freeze them; if this is the case it makes them easier to work with, especially if you only need part of one because you can shave off what you need with a knife and return the rest to the freezer before it thaws.

Habaneros and scotch bonnets are the same species (*Capsicum chinense*), and the two names often overlap. It tends to be that in the English speaking Caribbean they are referred to as scotch bonnets, and in the Spanish speaking Caribbean as habaneros (meaning resident of Havana). If you show the same chilli to a Jamaican and a Cuban they will both recognise it as something different and, for this reason, if you have a recipe that calls for one or the other, they are interchangeable.

Within the species there are hundreds of varieties, all characterised by their distinctive flavour and, usually, their heat. Some differ very little or only in colour, but some show other characteristics which lend themselves to particular purposes. There are some larger, more fleshy varieties, such as Antillais Caribbean or Big Sun, which are more juicy and great for sauce making but really don't dry very well at all. And others such as Paper Lantern, which are less succulent, have a longer shelf life, and are better for drying. For most recipes though, they are interchangeable and you can use whatever you have. They vary in heat from around 150,000 to 600,000 SHU.

For the grower these are much slower to mature than most chillies, but potentially very prolific. They benefit from tropical conditions, so a greenhouse or warm conservatory is ideal. If you see them for sale fresh, stock up, as they come and go in supermarkets, and from online sellers they are very seasonal. Put them in the freezer where they will keep almost indefinitely.

Hungarian Wax

Sometimes known as just wax chillies, banana chillies, or by a brand name such as 'Inferno' these are a collection of very versatile, crisp, mildly spicy (2,000 to 3,000 SHU) chillies that normally start off yellow, then turn red. In Hungary and Eastern Europe they are known by the general term, paprika, as when they ripen to red that is what they are used for. They are generally about 10-12cm long and have thin skins, so you don't need to remove the skins before eating them. They are one of the very easiest chillies to grow, and they are very versatile either as a cooking ingredient, or to grill and stuff, maybe with cheese.

Jalapeños

Jalapeños are probably the most widely recognised and popular chillies for both cooking and growing at home, and rightly so. They are versatile, tasty and easy to grow. They are sometimes available from supermarkets fresh and always available as pickled slices. You can buy small plants and seeds from garden centres and they are one of the easiest chillies to grow. As such this is probably one of the first chillies most people grow and the rewards can be great, treat them well and you will get a prolific supply for cooking, pickling and freezing from just one plant. They vary from about 6,000 to 10,000 SHU. Use them in salsas, for general chilli flavouring and for pizza topping.

Kashmiri

Whether or not you are keen on Indian or Kashmiri cooking you may wish to include this versatile Asian chilli in your collection. It is mild, around 2,000 SHU, so a lot of recipes call for quite a few of them in one dish, which of course imparts a lot of favour without the heat becoming overpowering. It also adds a lot of red colour. They are worth growing too if you can get hold of the seeds, but a lot of the dried ones you can buy have been dried at such a high temperature that the seeds are no longer viable.

Naga / Bhut Jolokia

Of the very hottest varieties, probably the most commonly available in dried and powder form is the bhut jolokia, or Naga jolokia, also known as ghost pepper. They have a heat level of around 1.1 million SHU, and used to be a record-holder, so they are not to be messed with. These are grown in Assam and Nagaland in North Eastern India where they are grown in the open fields in huge quantities. Other super-hot varieties may not be as easily available as they are not yet grown so prolifically. Some may dispute it but, with regard to flavour, most of these very hot ones are similar and therefore bhut jolokia can be used as substitutes for Trinidad Scorpion, Dorset Naga or Naga Morich. The use of these chillies is really reserved for the hottest of dishes and hot sauces where the heat and shock factor are most important. Otherwise, use them sparingly as a little goes a long way.

New Mexico Green and Red Chilli / Chile

I normally use the British spelling of the word chilli, that is my background, but when describing this one I feel I should take the opportunity to explain that in the USA the usual spelling is 'chile'. 'Green chile' is such a huge part of the culture of New Mexico that they would consider it an insult if I didn't at least explain myself. This is very much a product of the fields of New Mexico and Western Texas where they harvest 'green chile' by the ton, roast it by the roadside to remove the skins and sell it by the pound. It is used in large quantities for soup, stews, cold salads, rajas (roasted strips) or just eaten whole. The flavour is quite unique and worth experimenting with.

If you grow your own chillies then I would recommend you try 'Joe E Parker', the fruit is thick fleshed, they grow on a fairly big bush but the first chillies grow close to the stem so it is manageable.

There are others, New Mex 6-4, or Sandia (a hotter one) are two popular ones and you will find seeds for all of these through online seed merchants listed at the end of this book.

When picked green, these are fabulously tasty peppers, around 15-20 cm in length and with a firm, thick flesh. There is little heat in 'Joe E Parker' but they are so much more flavoursome than standard green sweet peppers. The downside is that these peppers all have thick skins which should be removed in the preparation process, but it is worth persevering, the rewards are great. On rare occasions the roasted green chillies are dried, at which point they become known as 'pasado'. Pasado, whole or powdered, is hard to come by but, if you grow your own and have a food dehydrator, you can make it yourself, a very worthwhile and rewarding experiment.

New Mexico Red

Much of the New Mexico crop is left to ripen to red at which point they are dried and sold whole, or ground into paprika. Despite paprika being of Hungarian origin, a lot of it is produced in the USA.

New Mexico is my standard 'red powder'. I have used plenty of it over the years. If you find it branded as 'New Mexico' mild or hot (hot is usually made from a variety called Sandia), this is generally an indication of quality and it will give lots of flavour and colour.

The hot version although branded as such, is still really quite mild, about 3,000 to 5,000 SHU. You can buy New Mexico powder from Mexican ingredient importers listed in the suppliers section at the end of this book.

If you have grown these, you can also dry your own. They dry well, though the process is hastened if they are left on the plant until they start to wrinkle.

Paprika and Smoked Paprika

are all examples of the types used to produce the powder. They ripen from a crisp yellow to red, then start to dry on the plant, at which point they are then picked, dried fully and ground to powder. In other parts of the world different varieties are used. A large proportion of the New Mexico crop goes towards paprika production, usually made from the 'New Mex 6-4', 'Joe E Parker' and related varieties, all well suited for drying.

The word paprika is a Hungarian word which describes a mild red chilli powder and the chilli from which it originates. The fresh chilli from which it is made can vary depending on where in the world it originates. In Hungary and Eastern Europe, varieties we know as Hungarian wax, hot wax or banana chilli

Paprika is used widely for flavour and colour in European cooking. In Spain, paprika, sometimes referred to as pimenton, is often produced from chillies which are smoked, producing a sweet smoky taste used to flavour dried cured meat.

Pasilla / Chilaca

Pasilla is the name for the dried version of the chilaca, a long (20 cm) dark brown chilli. When dried they appear black and look like twisted sticks of liquorice. They have some heat, around 2,000 SHU but they are used more for their flavour. They are a vital ingredient of many Mexican mole sauces and also give an intense flavour of prunes and liquorice. Fresh chilaca can be cooked whole and stuffed with cheese.

Pimiento de Padron

Pimientos de Padron are the small green chillies you see fried as tapas in Spain, they are delicious to eat, easy to cook and if you have the space for some big plants, and I mean up to 1.5 m tall, then these will provide a constant reward when picked young and fried with olive oil. There are details of how to cook them later in the book. The ones used for frying are picked immature, but if you leave them on the plant they grow into larger thin fleshed 10 cm long red fruits that are around 6,000 SHU which can be easily dried.

Piri Piri

Also referred to as peri peri or pili pili, this is a general name applied to African bird's-eye chillies of various types, though the name has been adopted into the Portuguese language too, through their involvement in African colonisation. These are pretty hot, from 80,000 SHU up to almost double that for some of the tiny ones, they range from 1 to 3 cm and are all members of the *Capsicum frutescens* species, so they are related to Thai, Brazilian Malagueta and Tabasco, and you can use these as substitutes in recipes if need be.

Serrano

Serrano is of Mexican origin and traditionally used in salsas in Mexico and the USA. They are not dissimilar in appearance to jalapeños, smaller and more slender, but slightly hotter at around 10,000 to 12,000 SHU.

They are easy to grow, but if you have limited space then they are interchangeable with jalapeño in most recipes so my advice would just be to stick with jalapeños.

Spanish Pimientos

Thick fleshed, almost like solid beef tomatoes, these provide a great source of flavoursome, red flesh for Spanish cooking and are great for stuffing with meat or vegetables. They are a great greenhouse pepper to grow, as they grow close to the stem on a compact plant.

Thai

There are hundreds of different types of chilli referred to as 'Thai', even someone from Thailand will have a different idea about what a true Thai chilli is; tiny, 1 cm super-hot little things, or 5 cm and slightly milder. The heat level can be up to 120,000 SHU. What they have in common is that they are of the species *Capsicum frutescens*, this makes them related to 'Tabasco', Brazilian malagueta and Zimbabwe bird chillies. They grow upright on the plant and, only in my opinion, the heat they have is felt at the front of the tongue and lips more than in the throat. You can enjoy experimenting to prove me wrong.

Trinidad Moruga Scorpion

I mention this by name as I find it one of the more reliable of the super-hot chillies to grow. In the past it has held the record for the hottest chilli, at over 1.2 million Scoville Heat Units (SHU). At the time of printing this record holder is the 'Carolina Reaper', but the title-holder changes frequently. These chillies are really the domain of more specialist growers and enthusiasts, they are outrageously hot, and therefore not to the taste of everyone, but for enthusiasts of hot sauces who wish to make their own, these or others like them are almost a necessity. They are expensive to buy and for the quantities needed to make a reasonable batch of sauce, growing your own is by far a cheaper option.

Complementary Herbs, Vegetables and Other Ingredients

Coriander (Cilantro)

You won't read far into this book before you realise that coriander is a frequent star in many of the recipes. Luckily you can buy fresh pots of it in supermarkets, and it is easy to grow; probably the easiest herb to cultivate on the windowsill, indoors or out.

Basil

This is another herb that could grace your kitchen window and reward you with its flavour. Fresh basil is so fragrant and adds so much more than the dried leaves ever could. Like coriander, it is well worth growing a handy pot of it if you can.

Epazote

Epazote is a Mexican culinary and medicinal herb often used to flavour beans. It is prolific and easy to grow, and in most climates it will grow outdoors once established and could even become a problematic weed, though it won't survive a UK winter. It has a pungent smell of creosote or paraffin and is used in small quantities as a flavouring, the side effect of which is to combat flatulence, a handy side effect for a flavouring used in beans. Use it sparingly.

Parsley

Maybe I am missing something, but dried parsley doesn't seem to compare to fresh. Unlike oregano, for example, where both dried and fresh have a place, I can't see when I would want to choose dried parsley over fresh. It isn't as pungent as oregano and the flavour doesn't intensify or change. So buy it fresh in pots, or grow your own; I choose to grow the flat leaved version it takes care of itself and doesn't go to seed as quickly as coriander.

Tomatillos

These are so easy to grow, even in temperate climates you can start them indoors and plant them into a vegetable patch or border in late spring. They will take care of themselves, ramble everywhere and look a bit untidy, but yield a crop of husk-bound green tomato-like fruits essential for making Mexican Salsa Verde and other dishes.

Manteca de Cerdo (Lard!)

In terms of healthy eating lard is probably as far down the bottom of the food spectrum as you can go, but it is something I use frequently so I thought I'd mention it. Making your own may sound like an unnecessary faff, but I only do it once in a blue moon, and I am always thankful that I have.

Lard you buy in shops is pure and filtered and white, but if you make your own you can retain the flavours of the meat. In Mexico it is referred to as 'manteca de cerdo', which I suppose translates as 'pig butter', usually prepared in such a way that it is golden, or at least so that you can separate the more desirable golden fat from the white stuff.

It is made by rendering your own pork fat. You can usually buy pork belly fat in a supermarket, a butcher will sell you some for next to nothing, or maybe even give it for free if you buy something else.

Firstly, put the fat in the freezer for half an hour, this will firm it up and make it much easier to work with.

Preheat your oven to gas mark 1, 275°F, 140°C.

Chop the fat into rough 2-4 cm pieces and put it in a lidded casserole dish with some water. The water will stop the fat from burning on the bottom of the dish.

Put it in the oven and leave for 4 hours or so. Stir it from time to time to help the fat break down, add a little more water if you think it is burning. When all or

most of the fat has melted and broken down, take the dish out of the oven and remove any lumps of skin and meat.

Leave the dish to cool. When the fat has solidified, spoon it into a freezer bag and freeze. The spoons of fat will stay roughly separate and you can use all or part of one whenever you need it.

For fans of pork scratchings, you can make use of the remaining skin by salting and baking it until it is dry and crispy, but this is an art I have yet to perfect, so I'm afraid I am unable to offer advice on the finer points of technique, though I continue to practice.

Achiote

This is primarily a food colouring made from the seeds of the annatto tree. It is blood red in colour, but imparts a yellow/orange colour to food and is commonly used in Central American cooking. It has a subtle flavour and I think it is less noticeable than turmeric, which is also used as a colouring, so I generally use it in preference unless a recipe relies on turmeric for flavour rather than colour. You can buy it from Mexican ingredient suppliers.

Preserving Chillies

CHAPTER 2

Preserving Chillies

Drying Chillies

Drying chillies has historically been the preferred method of preservation and in countries where they grow naturally outdoors this is a fairly easy process, just lay them in the sun or string them up in a warm breeze. If you are lucky enough to see chillies growing and drying in these circumstances one thing you will notice is that when they are laid out for drying, nature has already done a lot of the hard work. The chillies have been left on the plant to a point where they are already quite desiccated.

Types that are traditionally dried are grown in fairly arid areas where autumns are characterised by dry air and low humidity; Northern Mexico, New Mexico, Texas and the Peruvian Andes are examples of such places. The early season crop will have been picked to be used fresh, and at the tail end of the season, what is left will be dried. The plants will look well past their best, maybe crumpled and dying, and

the chillies are already beginning to shrivel when they are picked.

In the UK, Europe, and more temperate regions we may not have this advantage. We are forced into a choice of picking them crisp and fresh in the summer, or risk watching them go mouldy on the plant as the autumn sun dips lower in the sky and the cold, wet, rainy weather takes over. So for us the drying process takes a bit more thought.

So where does this leave us? Let's think about what chillies we want to dry. Thin-fleshed, long, small and dull-skinned chillies dry so much better than thick, fleshy, waxy ones. Habaneros and scotch bonnets don't dry well without some intervention; they have a waxy coating that means they will rot inside long before the skin allows water to escape, so they must be cut or broken open to allow moisture to escape.

This means the drying process needs to be quick, or they will spoil. The dried habaneros you buy will have been subjected to an industrial drying process which sees them crushed and conveyed through ovens to speed up the process.

The key to drying is warmth, low humidity and airflow. If you have radiators about the home you can hang your chillies off the top, or lay them across a double radiator. This is a quick method. Maybe you have a sunny window or an airing cupboard where you can lay them out on a drying rack? I have done this with skinny ones like cayenne or 'Ring of Fire', but it won't do for ancho or 'Joe E Parker', they are too fleshy.

When I started drying chillies a long time ago I built a drying box, a Heath-Robinson affair with tailor-made racks, a hot light bulb, tin foil reflectors and a fan; effective but fiddly, and probably a bit dangerous. You can still do this, but fortunately today there is a better option, a food desiccator. They have always been around, but until recently the processing capacity didn't justify the cost. Luckily now you can get your hands on one for as little as £30, definitely money well spent if you are planning on doing a lot of drying.

Once you have a food desiccator at your finger-tips your worries are over. Not only will it take care of easy-to-dry chillies, it will also act quickly enough for you to slice open the waxy moist ones and dry those too before they go mouldy, sometimes in just a few hours. This opens up a world beyond what is normally available to the cook and chilli enthusiast, anything you can grow or buy can be dried to give you a personal supply of chillies you could never hope to find from spice suppliers, and this will give you a much wider range of flavours to experiment with.

Storage and Rehydration

The optimum for dried chillies is not to make them crisp and crunchy, but slightly leathery and pliable. At this stage they will have lost enough moisture that they won't go mouldy, but they will retain their natural oils and therefore the flavour. They need to be stored in a dry airtight container away from light or they will go mouldy and lose their colour. They will keep for years this way.

Bringing your chillies back to life can be as easy as soaking them in hot water. A traditional Mexican cook will tell you to toss them in a dry frying pan first to warm them and bring out the natural oils, but this has never become a habit for me and I'm not sure what difference it makes. So just pour on some boiling water and leave them for 20 minutes or so before blending them to a paste or chopping them finely.

Chilli Powder

Once you have a supply of dried chillies in your cupboard you should also think about powder. Chilli powder will lose its flavour more quickly than whole dried, because it has a greater surface area and no outer protection, but powder is more versatile and easier to use, so consider keeping most of your stock as whole dried chillies, then making powder in small batches so you don't have to keep it more than a few weeks. This also enables you to blend different types and flavours in advance to make cooking your favourite dishes even easier.

Some purists consider using chilli powder as cheating, they think we should all be preparing dishes from whole dried chillies, toasting them lightly before use to release the flavours. Whilst this is technically correct, I don't subscribe to this ideal. Most of the time powder makes cooking so much easier and quicker, and therefore we are more inclined to do it.

Powder is easy to buy in all sorts of guises, but you may still want to make your own. The downside of making your own is that you definitely need a machine to do it, but they aren't expensive, a small spice grinder or cheap coffee grinder will do the job perfectly. Keep it separate for chilli grinding to avoid overheating your coffee beans. Once you have ground your powder keep it in an airtight container, small zip-lock bags are ideal, and try to squeeze all the air out if you can. Keep your powder in a dark place; it will lose its colour in a few days if it is left in the sunshine.

Chilli Flakes

For pizza topping, and as a visually appealing way of spicing up paella and rice dishes, you might need some chilli flakes too. This can be achieved in two ways. The easy way is to simply scrunch up your dried chillies into pieces. I don't really need to insult you by telling you that, but sometimes it isn't as easy as it sounds. Dried chillies should really retain some natural oils and not be bone-dry, so they don't always flake easily. Therefore you may need to dry them further in a low oven, or carry on your drying process to a point where they are crisp, then you can scrunch them by hand.

Making Ristras

An attractive way to dry and store chillies is to thread them into in what is traditionally called a 'ristra', the Spanish word for rope or string. In hot climates they can be strung up from fresh and left outside to be dried in the sun and wind. Whether or not you have the outside temperature and low humidity to do this is very much dependant on where you live. In the UK and Northern Europe you will struggle, especially at the end of the summer when most of your ripe chilli crop will be picked so you may find it better to dry your chillies first and then string them up for storage or decoration.

There are a couple of ways you can string your chillies. For small and lightweight chillies you can use a needle and strong nylon thread, piercing each one through the calyx (the green bit where the stem joins the top of the fruit). The other way is to use the string to tie a knot around each stem, or group of stems, to hold them into place. The second method doesn't work so well with fresh chillies, as the knot will loosen when the stem dries and shrinks and you stand a chance of them falling out.

If you want to string up fresh chillies I find the best way is to use the first method, the needle and thread, but do not push them together too tightly until they are dry. Leave them in an extended garland, then push them together tightly for display and storage when they are dry.

Smoking Chillies

Smoked chillies are probably something the enthusiast won't want to do without, you can buy them of course, but the selection is limited, and the prospect of smoking your own opens up a whole new world of flavours. Remember, you will be playing around with two groups of flavours, the chillies themselves and the different types of wood used to create the smoke. You can smoke any of your chillies, smoke the fresh ones and use them straight in cooking, smoke them and freeze them while still moist, or smoke them, then dry them to make 'chipotles'.

You will need to approach the smoking of chillies with an open mind, it is very much a process where the journey should be as enjoyable as the arrival, and be prepared for a few mistakes before your method is perfected. I have always found that the smoking of chillies is definitely an addictive and pleasurable one, much like making a good fire, and the more primeval the process, the more rewarding it becomes.

What Smoker to Use

My advice would be to start off cheaply, and work upwards, the spending of money is not a guarantee of success, and there is a greater reward to be had from producing sweet-tasting, oak-smoked chipotles that are tastier than anything you can buy, if you have done so without too much cost.

The various options open to you are:-

- Use a covered BBQ, either with wood chips and charcoal, or an off-the-shelf smoke generator

- Use a kitchen smoker with wood sawdust

- Use an old saucepan, with sawdust in the bottom, and sit a wire grill inside to hold the chillies

- Buy a large, fridge sized, electric smoker

- Build your own outdoor smoker

I have a small fire place with a chimney built in the garden which I use for smoking. I build a small charcoal fire on stones at the bottom then put a pile of sawdust on top which burns for a long time. The sawdust does need replenishing every couple of hours, but it means I can keep it running all day with minimum attention.

The most convenient method for most people is to use a BBQ with a closing lid, or if yours has no lid, then fashion one out of tin foil with a chimney hole to channel the smoke. Set a small pile of charcoal burning to one side of the BBQ, and then, when the charcoals are grey, smother them with sawdust which mostly extinguishes the fire but continues smouldering. Lay your sliced chillies on a rack on the other side of the BBQ so they aren't directly above the wood in case a fire flares up. Your job is then to make sure the burning sawdust doesn't extinguish entirely, but doesn't flare up either. You will find this BBQ method also helps to dry the chillies because the draw of the smoke rising up ensures a continuous flow of warm, dry air.

Another way is to use an old saucepan or tin supported above a tea light (small candle) and adapt a wire rack to fit inside to hold the chillies above a layer of sawdust. Slice the chillies onto the rack and keep a slight tilt on the saucepan lid to restrict the exit of the smoke. After a few goes at this you will perfect your technique and work out how long you need to smoke your chillies for in order to get the optimum flavour, but of course you are dependent on the candle, which will need replacing from time to time. This is a proven method for smoking all sorts of thing, but not something you can really do indoors, so you will need somewhere outside but sheltered so the candle doesn't blow out.

Purpose-Built Smokers

You can buy purpose built kitchen smokers, either electric or cooker-top, but they are primarily designed for smoking fish or meat for a short space of time. On the electric ones you can't set the timers for long enough to smoke chillies and they don't hold enough sawdust, so it means repeating the process over and over to get the intensity of smoke needed for chipotles.

Bigger smokers, the ones that look like fridges, are a huge investment, and don't necessarily do a better job than a home-made one. Because they are a sealed unit, they keep moisture in, and while moist meat or fish is desirable, you want a dry atmosphere for your chillies. If you are going to spend money, I would urge you to spend it on a smoke generator, a machine which pumps out a controlled stream of smoke which you can channel into a container of your own making for a fraction of the cost.

Wood and Sawdust

The type of wood you use will have a great influence on your end result and the flavours can be surprisingly diverse. Mesquite wood is often used in the USA and Mexico and you can buy this from specialist suppliers, but this does get expensive. In the UK, oak is an obvious choice, but apple and maple are others you might want to try.

You will need to get hold of some pure sawdust; this can be a challenge or part of the fun, depending on how you look at it. Only timber sawmills are likely to have an uncontaminated supply of decent sawdust or hardwood chips, carpentry workshops will have plenty but it is likely to be contaminated with chipboard, MDF or softwood dust. You may have to resort to buying sawdust or wood chips online, but you don't have to use the specialist pellets designed for purpose built smokers, so you can buy it loose and in bulk.

You can also add fresh herbs to the sawdust for an additional flavour.

Smoking Times and Temperatures

For most foods there are two styles of smoking. There is cold smoking, between 20-30 °C (68-76 °F) which just imparts the flavour of smoke, and hot smoking, between 50-80 °C (122-176 °F), where the food is not just smoked, but also slowly cooked. An hour of cold smoking is ok for mild chillies that are going to be cooked and eaten on their own, but for chipotles the process is slightly different; you want to impregnate them with enough smoke not only to flavour the chilli, but with a level of intensity that will add flavour to the dish to which you add your chillies. So you need to be thinking about smoking them for at least 6 hours. Also, you will want your chipotles to dry too, so a temperature somewhere between cold and hot smoking is best, and this is achievable with the methods described, though it won't dry them completely. In my experience, chillies of all kinds will need to be fully dried after smoking anyway, so baking them dry in your smoker shouldn't take priority over getting a good smoky flavour.

Be careful of going too hot, either through positioning the chillies too close to the burning sawdust, or allowing the fire to flare up. Cooking the chillies is fine, but if they start to turn to charcoal they will be bitter and unpalatable.

Preparing the Chillies

I think the only method of giving chillies a good smoky flavour in a domestic environment is to slice them open to allow the moist inside of the chilli to soak up the smoke. Without opening them to the smoke you will just coat the outside skin and you won't get anywhere near enough intensity. The fact that your chillies are now open to the elements means that they will need to be dried quickly, the smoke will help a little with their preservation but they will still go mouldy if they are left moist for too long. Refer to the chapter on drying chillies for more information.

Which Varieties are Good for Smoking?

I would say that if you have a setup that enables you to smoke chillies, then you should definitely experiment with anything you can get your hands on. Don't be afraid of breaking with the normal protocol of just smoking jalapeños, you will find a use for anything that comes out of your smoker, and they don't have to be dried before you can use them.

Once you have your smoker running you can do any of the following at the same time. For a good strong flavour you need to smoke things for up to 8 hours. But you can have a few types going at once, some milder strips for immediate consumption which you take out after an hour or so, and some that you leave for longer to make chipotles.

Jalapeños

Slice these into rings or strips, or to retain them whole make 4 slits down the side. They will soak up smoke a lot easier this way and give you the intensity of smoke you need for recipes that ask for chipotle. Smoke these for as long as you can, all day if possible.

Aji Limon

These are quite hot, so you aren't going to use an awful lot in your cooking at one time, you will still taste the smoke, and they work very well with fish because of their citrus flavour. Either dry them to make chipotles, or freeze them immediately after smoking.

Habanero

These are hotter still than the aji, but still soak up enough smoke provided you cut them open first. A nice thing to do with a smoked habanero is to freeze them after smoking rather than drying them, then you can defrost one and stir it straight into a pot of yoghurt with a chopped spring onion to make a hot smoky dip.

Red New Mexico or Hungarian Wax

When these are nice and ripe, slice them lengthwise and lay them out on the smoking rack. After drying they can be powdered into smoked paprika.

Freshly Smoked Strips

Grill and skin some larger chillies, such as poblano or pimentos, then lay strips of the partially cooked flesh onto the smoking rack and smoke them for an hour or so as you would fish. Then serve them as rajas according to the recipe later in this book. This is an opportunity to add herbs to your burning sawdust for an additional flavour.

Pickling Chillies

Pickling is not only one of the most common ways of preserving chillies; it is a popular way of enjoying them too. Pickled jalapeño slices and sweet cherry chillies are commonplace and easy to make at home.

Pickling is a method of preservation without refrigeration so there are some important considerations when it comes to cleanliness and sterilisation. The most important is to maintain a level of acidity in the finished product to prevent the growth of bacteria. As well as this we have to make sure that when preparing pickles, it is done in a way that removes or kills bacteria from the start.

This basic rule can be enforced by making sure that your pickling solution follows the basic recipe of a 50/50 water/vinegar solution, plus around 40g of salt per litre of liquid. This assumes that the vinegar you will use, regardless of type, will be around 5% concentration. If you follow the cooking guidelines below, this will guarantee to preserve your pickles, but may not make them particularly tasty or appetising to look at. So further to this there are the secondary considerations which are flavour, clarity of the solution, crispness of the end product, and making sure they maintain these properties for as long as possible.

There are some simple and obvious things you can do to improve the flavour, the most common being the addition of sugar to offset the sharpness of the vinegar, about the same amount of sugar as salt is a good start. You should also consider garlic, herbs or spices as ways of adding interest or enhancements to the flavour.

The type of salt you use will affect the look of your pickles, household salt contains iodine to stop it clogging together, this will cause the liquid to go cloudy, so go for sea salt without anti-caking agents or use pickling salt, made for exactly this purpose.

The type of vinegar you use will obviously affect the flavour, so you can choose whatever type you like but the use of malt vinegar should be avoided as it will soon discolour the chillies, turning them brown. Try white wine, cider, or rice wine vinegars for a nice flavour and good colour.

Maintaining Crispness

The crispness you find in commercially produced pickles is not difficult to recreate, but it does rely on the addition of an extra chemical. There are things you can do to minimise the softening of vegetables in pickles, such as using firm, fresh fruit from the start, and pickling them as soon as possible after slicing to avoid oxidisation, but the real crispness comes from the addition of calcium chloride, at around 1 teaspoon per litre. If you are hooked on those jars of small crunchy cherry chillies and want to make your own then this is the secret to their crispness, not the type of chilli they use. Likewise, with jalapeño slices it will stop them falling apart when you fish them out of the jar to top your pizza. Calcium chloride has an 'E number', E509, in that sense it is a food additive, but at least it is a safe one. You can safely leave it out of the following recipe, but you will miss out on crispness. It can be bought from home preserving or homebrew suppliers and is very cheap, but make sure you buy a food grade product not something used in aquarium keeping. There is a supplier listed at the end of the book.

Pickling Cherry Chillies or Jalapeños

I have already mentioned the small cherry-shaped chillies so many people are fond of, and recreating them yourself isn't too difficult as they are one of the easiest chillies to grow. If you grow them from seed there are dozens of different types to choose from, with a range of different heat levels and sizes, a specialist seed merchant will have a few different ones. Remember, regardless of what the manufacturer might tell you, it isn't so much the type of chilli that determines the end result of their commercial product, it is more about the crispness and the way in which they are preserved. The commercial ones substitute some of the vinegar for artificial preservatives, something you won't be able to do without laboratory testing to make sure you have a safe product, but this recipe comes close.

You will need some pickling jars with secure lids, either bought or saved. It can be difficult to estimate the size of jars and the volume of liquid you need. I do it by preparing the chillies, then filling the empty jars with them and then preparing a liquid mix of about 80% of the total volume of those jars. It is easier to overestimate the volume of liquid needed and throw a little away, than it is to make a second batch.

Ingredients

500g jalapeño chillies or small cherry chillies (or a mixture)

300ml water

300ml white wine vinegar

20g pure sea salt or pickling salt

30g white sugar

3/4 tsp calcium chloride

Method

- Place the jars and lids in a large saucepan of cool water and bring to the boil. Boil for 10 minutes then set aside for later.

- Add all the ingredients, except the chillies, to another saucepan, and bring to the boil.

- Slice up your jalapeños and discard the stalk end, or for cherries slice off the top and scoop out the seeds with the handle of a spoon.

- Take the jars from the hot water using tongs and oven gloves. Drain them of excess water and stuff the chillies into them up to just below the rim.

- Pour in the hot pickling mixture to cover the chillies (some may float to the top), stir them to allow excess air to escape, then seal the jars.

- Return the sealed jars to the saucepan of hot water and return to the heat. Boil for a further 10 minutes. This won't be the case in the UK, but if you live at high altitude (over 6,000 ft), you should extend this time to 15 minutes.

- Leave the finished product for at least two weeks before you start to eat them, though they should last up to two years.

- Of course you can vary the content of this recipe hugely, as long as the pickling mixture stays the same. Try flavouring mild chillies with a few pieces of something hotter, and add garlic or herbs for extra flavour. You can pickle slices of bigger chillies or peppers, or whole piri piri. If you use tiny ones, pickle them whole with stalks, but slice them down one side to allow the pickling mixture to get inside.

Freezing

Freezing chillies is by far the easiest way to keep them for long periods of time. They won't lose their flavour. They don't need to be peeled, chopped or blanched. When you want to use them there isn't usually a need to pre-thaw them. Mostly they can be chopped from frozen or just left to thaw for a minute. When you chop them from frozen they will usually crumble into pieces. There is no real limit to how long you can keep them for in the freezer. I have kept them for years without any loss of flavour or heat.

Honey

means of keeping a few chillies for use in sweet dishes, and the flavoured honey becomes as important as the chilli it is preserving. Later in this book is a recipe for grapefruit salad, and this is a perfect use for chillies in honey. I normally keep a jar of honey with a few habanero chillies in it for just such purposes.

Only use good quality, clean chillies. Slice them open to allow the honey to infuse and drop them into a part-used jar of honey (overflowing a full jar will be a little messy). Poke them around a bit to make sure all the air is released. Leave them for at least a couple of weeks, but they will store for months or even years. The sugar in the honey draws out the moisture from the chillies leaving them looking slightly shrivelled and translucent, but with the colour still intact.

Because honey is a naturally occurring product it has been a part of the food of mankind since the start of our existence, and its qualities as a preservative have probably been exploited for almost as long. It isn't really a practical means of preserving large amounts of surplus crop but, never the less, it is a fun and useful

You can use all or part of a chilli, and the honey too, as long as you leave enough to keep the remaining chillies submerged.

Chillies in Alcohol

Habanero Vodka

This one is the real deal. A bonfire night special to shock your friends, a game of Russian roulette, or for something milder mix it in fruity cocktails. The habanero does impart an amazing flavour but the heat, and the way the heat permeates every part of you, will be seriously intense. Have some yoghurt handy.

Ingredients

1 half bottle of vodka
1 large red habanero or scotch bonnet chilli (can be from frozen)

A red habanero, particularly something fleshy like an Antillais, will also give a nice pink glow to the vodka. But it is the fruity flavour you are really after, so any colour will do.

Slice the chilli into small enough pieces to fit into the bottle neck and drop them in. This won't need to sit for very long before the flavour and heat permeates the alcohol. A couple of hours at the most will do it.

This drink really will seem hotter than the chilli on its own, and proves once and for all that trying to combat a chilli burn by washing it down with an alcoholic drink is not the way to go. The vodka reaches parts you never knew existed, all the way down to your stomach. Don't forget the yoghurt.

For a milder experience, drinking this vodka with orange or pineapple juice really does show off the habanero flavour. Give it a go.

Aji Crystal Vodka - a Milder Alternative

I have to admit I am not a fan of super strength chilli vodka, or any very spicy spirit for that matter, but there is room to warm my heart with a more flavoursome combination, and this one is certainly that.

This is made using a dried aji crystal chilli, you can get these or the closely related aji amarillo from dried chilli suppliers or grow your own. They aren't too hot, and have a slight citrus taste.

Ingredients

1 half bottle of vodka

1 dried aji amarillo chilli

Method

- Slice the chilli open lengthways four times from tip to just below the top, This will give it four 'legs' which separate when it starts to rehydrate and allow the vodka to rinse the flavours from inside.

- Rinse the chilli quickly in cold water to remove any dust or loose seeds. The finished product looks a bit cleaner and crisper with as few bits floating around as possible.

- You need to make space for the chilli, so pour yourself half a measure of vodka as a reward for getting this far through such a complicated recipe.

- Push the chilli into the neck of your vodka bottle, it should just fit.

- Leave it for at least a day. The colour quickly leaches out into the spirit to give it the look of tequila or malt whisky and the chilli itself will turn a translucent golden colour.

As a variation I have used a smoked chilli, an oak-smoked one, which of course imparts a toasted oak flavour, very nice.

Chilli Sherry

Chilli sherry is a traditional seasoning for soup and creamy sauces or as a remedy for a blocked nose or sinuses. I think that sherry deserves a hotter chilli than vodka, as it is used to impart heat and flavour to another dish, so I maintain the tradition and use small piri piri chillies from Portugal.

As sherry has a lower alcohol content than vodka it needs steeping for longer to get the most out of the chilli. You can use dried or fresh chillies for this recipe; there is no danger of fresh chillies rotting, as there is with oil, because the alcohol prohibits growth of bacteria.

Ingredients

1 bottle medium sherry (use dry sherry if you prefer but I think it needs a slight sweetness).

8 piri piri chillies (alternatively use 2 habaneros or scotch bonnets for a hotter, fruitier flavour)

Method

- Slice the piri piri up from the tip to below the stalk to allow the sherry inside.

- As with the vodka you will need to take a break from such a complicated procedure so take a tot of the sherry as a reward, this also makes space for the chillies in the bottle.

- Drop the chillies into the bottle, give it a shake and leave it for at least a fortnight. Have a taste to make sure it is ok.

You can vary the chilli content, I met a man who half fills the bottle, but that will make for a very potent brew.

Chillies in Oil

There is only one very important rule to remember when making chilli oil, and that is to use only dried chillies.

Oil is not a method of preserving fresh chillies. Even though you are starving them of air, they still contain moisture and therefore they can rot anaerobically (without air). The bacteria that cause this rot is botulism, which can be deadly. So if you use fresh chillies you must refrigerate the oil as though it is a perishable product. This should be common knowledge but after many years of advising on the preservation of chillies I still come across people who assume that they can stuff fresh chillies in bottles of oil and sit them in the cupboard for months.

This is the only rule you need to abide by, after that you can play around to your heart's content, different oils, different chillies, dried herbs, and any combination thereof.

If you are putting whole chillies in a bottle of oil make a small hole at the bottom and top of the fruit to allow air to escape. This will allow the oil to infuse and the chilli to release the flavour and heat. Allow the oil to sit for at least a couple of weeks, longer if possible, to maximise the flavour. You can speed the process up slightly by warming the oil, but be very careful not to overheat it as this will result in a burnt taste; I would just be patient.

Skinning Your Chillies

If you grow, buy and cook larger chillies and intend preparing them whole and fresh, as opposed to drying them, you will need to perfect your skinning technique. The skin of poblano and New Mexico chillies in particular is quite thick, almost like cellophane and makes for an unpalatable ingredient in an otherwise delectable mouthful, even if it is in small pieces.

Skins can be a bit fiddly to remove, but once you have perfected your own way of doing so it shouldn't take long. The idea is to somehow sear the whole chilli until the skin bubbles and separates from the flesh, but doing so without fully cooking the flesh so it still maintains some structure. There are various methods; grilling, baking, a BBQ, the open flame of a gas ring, or a blow torch. My preferred method is

a combination of grilling, and turning them in the open flame of a gas ring with tongs. This way I can ensure that the tip, the shoulder and every crease or fold is evenly heated. If you watch closely you will see the skin bubble and pop as steam forms underneath.

Place them on a tray under the grill and wait for them to start popping as the skin blisters. The smell will be mouth-watering. Turn them and shuffle them around so that as much of their surface is exposed to the grill as possible. Once they are hot and partly done, take each one in turn and hold it with tongs over a naked gas flame if you have such a thing. Pay special attention to the parts the grill hasn't reached, probably the top and any creases.

Once they have evenly blistered leave them to cool to a point where you can handle them. Putting them in a plastic bag for this time will help with the

peeling process, but you will eventually become proficient enough at blistering the skins to remove them without having to resort to the bag. Poblano skins are a little thinner and tend to burn more easily; they can be fiddly, but try rinsing them under a tap to help wash off the pieces.

CHAPTER 3

Sauces and Preserves

Sauces and Preserves

The sauces and preserves in this chapter are those that are preserved by their ingredients to give them a long shelf-life, allowing them to be stored in their bottles and jars at room temperature with no danger of them spoiling. Later on, Chapter 4 deals with sauces and pastes that do not enjoy a long life, and therefore need to be consumed immediately, or refrigerated.

General Hot Sauce Making Tips

There is something to bear in mind before you embark on your new career as a sauce maker, and that is the rules of preservation; making sure your sauce won't go mouldy or ferment, ruining the flavour or, worse still, poisoning somebody. Taking heed of these simple rules will mean that your sauce will have a lifespan of months or years, rather than days, and won't need to be refrigerated.

There are three factors and ingredients you want to consider when it comes to preservation of sauce.

Firstly, acidity; this is one of the keys to sauce preservation as it stops bacteria growing. Bacteria and yeast won't grow in a liquid if it reaches a certain level of acidity, a pH level of 3.9. You could buy a special meter to measure this level, and adjust your ingredients accordingly, but this isn't really necessary as long as at least 1/3rd of your recipe is vinegar of some kind. You can substitute some of the vinegar for lime or lemon juice, as this too, is acidic. If you want to start refining your ingredients, or move away from using vinegar, you can use an artificial acidity regulator such as citric acid powder, but once you delve into the realms of food additives you will need to be a bit more scientific and start measuring pH to make sure you get it right.

Secondly, sugar; bacteria and mould always need moisture i.e. water to grow; this is why completely dry ingredients don't go mouldy. Sugar has a special chemical property which means that it bonds with water, making that water unavailable for bacteria to use. So sugar acts as a preservative, think of how jam doesn't go mouldy, except maybe on the surface. This is because of its high sugar content.

Thirdly, salt; salt prohibits the growth of bacteria and yeasts, therefore the addition of salt will also help in the preservation process. Too much salt isn't always desirable, but for extremely hot sauces, where only a drop or two are used to spice things up, a high salt content won't be noticeable.

Hopefully this helps explain the importance of some of the ingredients in the following recipes.

Settling and Separation

You will probably find that, to a greater or lesser degree, your bottled sauces will settle so that some of the ingredients sink or float. This is quite natural, and doesn't necessarily affect the flavour; it is just less visually appealing and may be seen as less professional looking. Most of the sauces you buy in the shops only maintain their even consistency through the addition of artificial stabilisers or thickening agents such as guar gum or xanthan gum. Using these ingredients is a little beyond the hobby sauce-maker, so you need to use some other tactics to try and minimise settling out of your ingredients.

Firstly, the balance of ingredients needs to be right. Obviously, if a sauce is too watery the ingredients are more likely to settle, but too thick and the sauce won't pour properly. Try to strike a balance.

Secondly, emulsification; this is a key to maintaining a consistent sauce. Emulsification means breaking down the ingredients to such small particles that they are no longer heavier than water and therefore remain in suspension. In a commercial sauce making operation this might mean using an emulsifying machine which forces the sauce through tiny holes at very high pressure. If you have ever tried to make tomato ketchup at home you will appreciate how difficult it is to emulate the emulsification process. Emulsification is a very exact science; too small and the result might taste oily; too big and the ingredients will settle, which is why commercial sauces also use additives to help with the job.

At home you can try and do your best to achieve smoothness in two ways; extending the cooking time by letting it simmer for longer, and extending the blending time. Both these processes will help to break down larger particles into smaller ones.

Bottles and Jars

Sterilisation

Bottles and jars need to be clean, dry and free of any solid contaminants such as dust or remains of the previous contents. This is a particular challenge if you use recycled jam jars and sauce bottles. They should first be washed in hot, soapy water and rinsed, or put through a dishwasher. To ensure complete sterilisation you can sit them submerged in a large saucepan and boil them for 15 minutes. Alternatively, lay them on a tray in an oven preheated to gas mark 1, 275°F or 130°C and bake them for 15 minutes.

Breakages

If you get to the stage where you are bottling a lot of sauce in one go, and many people do, you need to be mindful of chipping the glass. Keep your bottle-handling area away from your cooking area and bring your cooked sauce to the bottles when you are ready. Check the rims of your bottles before you start washing them, discard any that are damaged. Then inspect them again before you put the funnel in to start filling. Unfortunately if you do then notice a chip, this has obviously occurred during the cleaning process and there is only one way to deal with the problem. That is to discard the broken one and go back to the start and re-wash everything. You must rinse them upside down to make sure a potential glass chip doesn't stick with surface tension to the inside of a bottle.

Filling Bottles and Jars

For preserved sauces and jams there is a requirement for your liquid to be over 82°C at the point of bottling, this is an additional safety measure to kill off airborne bacteria when the jar or bottle is sealed. In the absence of a food thermometer you can be fairly sure that if your liquid was at a rolling boil, and you remove from the heat and bottle it within a minute or two, then you will be safe. Fill your bottles to 1cm below the rim; the liquid will shrink as it cools. After screwing on the lid you should then invert your jars or bottles so the liquid helps sterilise the inside of the lid.

You will always hear warnings that jars and bottles should not be filled cool because of the danger of them shattering. I have experimented with this thoroughly, both in a food factory environment and at home. Only very, very, rarely does this happen. Modern, consistent glass manufacturing processes have helped here. My recommendation would be that glass should be at least warm not freezing cold, and if you are using the oven or boiling water method of sterilisation then they certainly will be, but there is no need to use glass straight from the oven or pan, it is safer to leave them to cool down to a manageable level before handling them.

Be Careful

Needless to say, the preparation of hot sauces and preserves means you are handling some very hot and dangerous liquids in a way that you would not do during normal cooking. Boiling sugar and vinegar are much hotter than boiling water, and sugary liquids stick to the skin. Be very careful when filling bottles with a funnel not to knock them over; wear a sturdy apron and gloves if necessary.

Basic Chilli Sauce Recipe

A basic chilli sauce is the easiest thing in the world to make, and if you use a single variety of chilli they are a great way to illustrate its flavours and characteristics. If your hobby develops, inevitably you will be drawn into experimentation with the blending of different chillies and other ingredients to stamp your own signature on the sauces you make.

Ingredients

250g chillies
125ml water
125ml white wine vinegar or cider vinegar
10g salt

You can adjust the quantity of chillies used, and proportionally reduce the other ingredients, but beware that if you reduce the quantities too much then evaporation of liquid during the cooking process will mean the sauce thickens very quickly, resulting in something so soupy that it won't pour well after it is bottled.

Method

- Cut the stems off of the chillies and roughly chop them into pieces. You are handling a lot of chillies here and you may want to use gloves to avoid having to suffer the after effects of having chilli juice all over your hands.

- You can add all the ingredients to a saucepan together, bring them to the boil and simmer until the chilli pieces have softened. Then the sauce will need blending, either in a blender or in the pan with a stick blender.

- If you bottle this according to the earlier guidelines it will preserve well for months or longer.

Chilli Lime Sauce

This is a deliciously sharp sauce with a Caribbean feel to it, and really easy to make. I look upon it as a ceviche sauce, because it has the same flavours as the raw fish dish 'cooked' in lime juice. It gives plain fish of any kind a real zest; fillets, crab meat, shellfish, anything that comes out of the sea will sing with a splash of this.

You can use any colour chilli, orange or red look a little more appetising, but if you are struggling to use up some green ones then these will complement the name by giving a greenish colour.

Ingredients

100ml white wine vinegar
100ml water
Juice of 4 limes
3 habanero chillies, finely chopped
125g jam sugar
3 cloves of garlic, finely chopped
2cm cube fresh ginger, finely chopped

Method

- This is the simplest of recipes to make. Mix all the chopped ingredients with the liquids and the sugar together in a small saucepan. Squeeze in as much of the lime juice and insides as you can and bring to the boil. The chopped pieces need to be as fine as you can get them. If you are tempted to blend the sauce to achieve this you can, but do so before it boils, so much safer than splashing boiling sugar all over yourself. I tend to use frozen habaneros for things like this, they break down much more easily when you chop them.

- You can use normal sugar, but jam sugar is easily available and contains pectin, a substance that occurs naturally in apple cores and unripe fruit which helps jam set. In this instance it helps to thicken the sauce slightly and stops the ingredients sinking so much.

- When the sauce has boiled transfer it to bottles for later use. It is a preserved sauce and if you follow the guidelines in the section on bottling then it will keep for months at least.

Mango Habanero Sauce

This fruity recipe will make what most people would consider to be a hot West Indian or Belize-style sauce. Some aficionados will think it is a little weak though, so there is no harm in adding more chillies, even doubling or tripling the number of chillies used without changing the quantities of the other ingredients.

Ingredients

200g mango

100g grated carrot (preferably small or baby carrots)

100g white onion, chopped

50g white sugar

5 x orange or yellow habanero or scotch bonnet chillies

150ml water

200ml cider vinegar

2 cloves of garlic, chopped

1cm cube fresh ginger, chopped

½ tsp salt

Method

- Use baby carrots if you can get hold of them, or at least small ones that aren't woody and tough. If you are using fresh mango, remove the flesh and chop it into pieces. One large mango should do, but buy two just in case, you can eat the leftovers. You can alternatively use a tin of mango pieces; if you do so, use the stuff tinned in juice rather than syrup, a 400g tin should give you just over 200g of flesh with a few pieces left as a snack.

- Chop the onion, garlic, ginger and chillies and grate the carrot. Add to a pan with the salt, water, mango pieces, vinegar and sugar. Bring to the boil and simmer with the lid on for about 30 minutes. Keep an eye on it, don't let the mixture boil dry or thicken beyond a watery slush, add a little more water if need be.

- The mango should break down quite quickly, and eventually the onion will soften too. Transfer to a blender and blend this mixture to a smooth thick creamy liquid. Alternatively use a stick blender to do this in the saucepan. Don't be shy, you are after a perfectly smooth finish and you can't blend it too much; the more you do it the less likely the sauce is to separate into solid and liquid. If you use a separate blender, rinse your saucepan while it is empty, you will be returning the mixture to boil again so you need to make sure that stray lumps don't mess up your smoothness. You may find there are some persistent stringy mango threads too, so remove these using a fork, they probably won't break down much further and will only clog up your bottles.

- If the liquid looks too thick, you can add a little extra water during the final simmer. Remove from the heat and bottle according to the earlier instructions.

Brazilian Molho Malagueta Table Sauce

This is a standard table sauce in parts of Brazil, a hot vinaigrette that is splashed over all sorts of things, much as we would do with tomato ketchup. The fresh chillies used are preserved by the acidity in the vinegar, although they sit in oil too.

The Malagueta chilli is a native of Brazil and had a distinctive flavour. The closest match is the Zimbabwe bird chilli, which also grows on a fairly tight but large bush and also has tiny pointed chillies less than 1 cm long. Obviously any small chilli can be used but you will need to adjust the quantity of chillies if you go for something larger, so if you choose to use Twilight I would halve the number to 50.

Ingredients

½ ltr glass bottle (an old olive oil or vinegar bottle with built-in pourer would be great).

200ml white wine vinegar

200ml olive oil

100 malagueta chillies (use any small bird's-eye type as substitute)

A few shavings of sliced onion

Method

- This is as simple to make as stuffing chillies in a bottle; this is the way it was traditionally made. I am always super keen to make sure that things are sterile and will last without rotting so I say the chillies should be steeped in the vinegar first before you add the oil. It is difficult and time consuming to slice open tiny Malagueta chillies as they are so small, so crushing them slightly with the side of a knife will split them to allow the vinegar in, and the flavours out. Put them into a bottle with the onion and vinegar, leave them for a few hours and add the oil later. This ensures you don't end up with fresh chillies floating in the oil and rotting.

Sweet Red Onion Sauce

This is a versatile and addictive sweet chilli sauce. When bottled, it will keep for a long time, though you will rarely allow it to do so. Add it to stir-fries, rice, mashed potato, or as a dipping sauce for prawns and barbecued meat.

Ingredients

250g red onions, chopped

150ml cider vinegar

300ml water

200g white sugar

1 fresh habanero chilli, chopped (can be from Frozen)

4 cloves of garlic, chopped

1 tsp piri piri or Thai chilli powder or flakes (or substitute with something hot and red)

Method

- Add the onions, garlic and chilli to a saucepan with the 300ml of water and simmer slowly with the lid on for 20 minutes to soften the onions, the liquid will reduce during simmering, probably to around 200ml.

- Tip the mixture into a blender and reduce it to a smooth broth.

- Return to the saucepan with the vinegar, sugar and chilli powder and bring to the boil, simmer for a couple of minutes. Be very careful at this stage, do not leave your saucepan unattended, the sugary solution can overflow in seconds as soon as it starts to boil. Be ready to turn down the heat or remove the pan in order to control the temperature.

- Because of the sugar and vinegar, this boiling mixture is much hotter than boiling water, so you need to be very careful, let it cool for a couple of minutes in the pan before you funnel it into bottles because of the danger of cracking the glass. It will still be a high enough temperature to help sterilise the bottles.

- Fill the bottles to within 1cm of the top. The liquid will shrink slightly as it cools.

Ancho, Blackberry and Port Sauce

This is a seasonal sauce in every sense; made in the summer at a time when you can enjoy the rewarding pleasure of blackberry picking and consumed in the winter with roast game and Christmas dinner. It has the balance of ingredients to give it a long shelf-life, so making it in the summer for winter consumption is quite ok, though that isn't to say you can't use it on barbecued meat or a fried breakfast.

This has, and probably always will be, my favourite hot sauce; unfortunately the cost and availability of the ingredients always prohibited making it on a commercial scale, though I do remember selling an experimental batch in farmers markets at Christmas time in 2003, for years afterwards people would ask for it again.

Ingredients

200ml port

300g blackberries

125ml red wine vinegar

30g ancho chilli powder

75g light brown sugar

Juice of 1 small orange

2 fresh habanero chillies

½ tsp salt

Method

- The plumper and sweeter your blackberries the better; rinse and drain them. Add all the ingredients, except the sugar, together in a small saucepan and bring to the boil for a slow simmer. The blackberries will start to break down, but give them a helping hand with a potato masher or a stick blender. Simmer slowly for 10 minutes. Once the blackberries have broken down you will need to push the sauce through a sieve into a second saucepan to remove the pips. In the second saucepan, now containing all but the pips and a few skins, add the sugar and bring back to the boil.

- Once the sugar has dissolved turn off the heat and bottle as described at the start of this section.

- All sauce making can get a bit messy, but be especially careful with this one; there is a lot of purple stuff in it, and it is likely to stain everything soft or absorbent that it comes into contact with.

Super-Hot Naga Sauce

Firstly, you need to make sure your extractor fan is functioning properly. The making of this sauce isn't a comfortable process.

Regardless of their level of heat tolerance, it is likely that the keen chilli-grower will be drawn to experiment with the hotter varieties, and when this happens the inevitable result is a glut of chillies so hot that the crop from one plant will last for years. You can sometimes buy naga, bhut or Trinidad scorpion chillies, but that is an expensive way to make this sauce as they don't usually come cheap. But if you can get hold of the ingredients this is a worthwhile way of making use of them. This sauce will last a long time, it is a great flavour, and it will impress your friends.

This recipe employs a technique which not only makes the sauce hotter by cramming more heat into the bottle, but also helps to stop it settling out, and that is to use powder as well as fresh. When chillies dry, their weight and volume is reduced dramatically through moisture loss, whilst still retaining heat and flavour. This enables you to cram more into the bottle than you ever could if you were just using fresh chillies, 20g of powder is equivalent to around 120g of fresh; terrible.

Ingredients

10 fresh Naga, bhut jolokia, Trinidad scorpion or similar

150ml white wine vinegar

100g mango pieces in juice (drained weight)

100ml water

20g Naga powder (or similar, as above)

4 cloves of garlic

25g brown sugar

1 tsp salt

¼ tsp ground cloves

¼ tsp ground nutmeg

Method

- Chop the tops off the fresh chillies and add them to a blender with all the other ingredients. Blend them as smooth as you can, then transfer to a saucepan and simmer the sauce over a low heat. Simmer for at least 10 minutes. The mango in this sauce will help it hold its consistency once bottled. It might benefit from a second blend after it has cooked if you can stand it.

- This is a preserved sauce which will keep for a long time if you follow the earlier instructions on how to bottle it safely.

Some Tips on Handling Super-Hot Chillies

Depending on your outlook on life the experience of cooking a big batch of super-hot sauce like this can either be something to laugh about, or one of the worse decisions you ever made. Ventilation is key, if you can do it outside on a camping stove with a fresh breeze blowing then you might get away with it, indoors you might want to consider a gas mask, and not one of those cheap dust masks either, you are dealing with gas, not dust (until you start powdering them!).

I bet you've read the often repeated tip in cookery books 'use gloves when chopping chillies'. And I bet your retort is probably something like 'Nah, don't need those'. Well in this case you certainly do, really, you do. And some goggles or at least a pair of glasses wouldn't go amiss either. Remember, looking closely at the inside of chillies and seeing the golden coloured capsaicin cells along the strip that bears the seeds? Well in these super-hot chillies the whole inside is covered with that stuff. It sprays out when you chop them, and gets absolutely everywhere.

- When you are washing up, use cold water first, you don't want a blast of hot steam in your face, or put things in a dishwasher

- Use medical or rubber gloves. Wash the gloves whilst still wearing them

- Blend things whilst still cold if you can, rather than while they are boiling

- If you are grinding your own powder, definitely use a dust mask

- If you are a regular at this a gas mask might be a worthwhile investment

Pineapple and Jalapeño Chutney

A tropical sweet and sour chutney that goes great with cold meats, and also popadoms and curry. It is quite a hot one, and you will pick up the distinct flavours of the jalapeño and the habanero.

Ingredients

1 pineapple (750g of flesh)

8 green jalapeño chillies, around 200g

250ml white wine vinegar

150g brown sugar

100g red onion, chopped

2 cloves of garlic, chopped

2cm cube of fresh ginger, chopped

1 fresh habanero chilli, chopped

1 tsp salt

½ tsp ground cinnamon

Method

- This is an easy one to make; all the ingredients can go in together, and don't worry about chopping the pineapple in a tidy fashion, it will break down in the cooking process. At first it will seem there isn't enough liquid but the pineapple will soon release its juices when the mixture starts to heat. Simmer it, probably for at least an hour or so, stirring occasionally. Eventually it will start to thicken and when the liquid that settles on the top as it cooks becomes syrupy, you can rely on the fact that it will have the right consistency when it cools.

- Transfer to sterile jars according to earlier instructions.

Chilli Jam

This is one of the most popular and tasty things that chilli lovers ask for, though this recipe could almost be considered a bit of a cheat, as it doesn't really have that much hot chilli in it, the bulk of it being made up of red peppers and red onion. However it is completely addictive and after you have tried this you will be craving it forever more.

It is simple to make, and you can knock up a kilo jar of it in half an hour. It is the perfect accompaniment to cheese, fried liver, smoked mackerel, peanut butter sandwiches, and just about anything savoury.

This recipe makes enough to fill a 1kg jar

Ingredients

500g red peppers

175g red onion, chopped

500g jam sugar

2 fresh habanero chillies, chopped

Juice of 2 lemons

Method

- You can buy jam sugar in supermarkets alongside normal sugar. Peppers and onions don't contain as much pectin as sharper fruits, and jam sugar contains additional pectin which makes a big difference in this recipe. It is a natural extract that makes the end product a bit more jelly-like, rather than runny. Having said that, you can use normal sugar and it won't affect the taste, it will just be slightly runny.

- Firstly, place a small plate or saucer in the refrigerator; you will need it later to test whether your jam is properly cooked or not.

- You also need to sterilise a jar (or jars), ready to take the boiling mixture. Refer to the earlier section on bottles and jars for instructions on how to do this.

- Remove the stems and seeds from the peppers, chop these finely and add them, with the other ingredients to a large saucepan, preferably a broad one with a thick base; the mixture will benefit from a wide surface area to allow quick evaporation.

- Bring to the boil, stirring all the time. Be careful of this hot liquid, it is much hotter than just boiling water and sticks like glue. Keep stirring regularly; you are looking for the liquid to reduce in volume, enough for it to set correctly. This will probably take about 15 minutes. In-between stirs, allow the jam to froth. Eventually the froth will start to turn from pale beige to a pinky colour.

- At this time take a teaspoon of the liquid and drop it onto your cold plate, after about 30 seconds it should set, and take on the consistency of a jelly with a slight skin on top, rather than a runny liquid. If not, keep cooking and try again in a couple of minutes.

- When the jam is ready, you can just pour it into your jar (or jars). As long as the jars are clean and airtight this should keep for months or more at room temperature. Happy eating!

CHAPTER 4

Pastes and
Fresh Sauces

Pastes and Fresh Sauces

Green Chimichurri – Argentinian Steak Sauce

Chimichurri is a table accompaniment to grilled meat in Argentinian cooking. Argentinians are great meat eaters, and particularly beef. There are many local variations of this recipe but the predominant ingredients are the parsley and oregano. You can vary this recipe by using red wine vinegar, or substituting part of the vinegar measure with a small proportion of balsamic vinegar.

Serves 4 as an accompaniment to steak.

Ingredients

25g chopped flat-leaf parsley

15g fresh oregano (or marjoram)

1 spring onion

3 cloves of garlic

40ml white wine vinegar

60ml extra virgin olive oil

½ tsp salt

1 green jalapeño chilli

Method

- Prepare at least an hour or two in advance of cooking your meat. Remove any thick stems from the parsley and the oregano and chop them finely, along with the spring onion, chilli and garlic. Use all the leaves of the spring onion too. Mix them in a bowl with the vinegar, oil and salt. Leave to steep in the fridge for a couple of hours and stir again before serving. If you make a large batch by doubling the quantities you can freeze some for later use.

Chipotles in Adobo Sauce

Chipotles, as explained earlier in more detail, are smoked chillies, usually jalapeños, which are dried to fully preserve them. They are a vital ingredient in lots of Mexican recipes, and preparing them in advance in a flavoursome sauce, called adobo, is a versatile way of making sure you have them to hand. The simplest use of them is to chop up one of them and mix it with yoghurt for a tasty dip.

Most dishes that ask for chipotles in adobo ask for 1-2 chipotles, so this recipe will give enough for 6-12 dishes. The rest can be refrigerated or frozen for later use.

Ingredients

13 chipotle morita chillies

250ml boiling water

50g onion, chopped

150ml cider vinegar

1 tsp honey

200g fresh tomatoes

2 cloves of garlic

½ tsp salt

Method

- Put the 13 chipotles in a bowl and cover with the boiling water, leave them to soak for 20 minutes while you prepare the other ingredients. Finely chop the onion, garlic and tomatoes and add to a saucepan, along with the honey, salt and vinegar. Stir the chipotles in the hot water occasionally to make sure they all rehydrate fully.

- When soft, take one of the chipotles and chop it finely before adding it with the other 12 whole ones to the pan.

- Bring to the boil, and simmer very slowly for an hour or so. Keep an eye on it, stirring occasionally, and add a little extra water if the mixture starts to thicken too much. As the mixture simmers the chipotles will hold their form, while the rest of the ingredients boil down to a fairly thick sauce which will thicken further on cooling.

- This can then be refrigerated in a bowl or jar for a couple of weeks, or frozen. It is likely that you will only need one or two chillies at a time so if you are going to freeze it, either separate into small portions, or lay it thinly in a tray so you can break it up into pieces once frozen.

Red Pepper Pesto

Remember, the boundary between what is a chilli and what is a pepper is very fuzzy, ill-informed opinions will tell you one thing or another but the truth is that a supermarket pepper, red, green, yellow or any colour for that matter comes from the plant species *Capsicum annuum*. This is the same species as the un-named red chillies that sit next door on the supermarket shelf, the same species as jalapeños, paprika, Romano peppers, and hundreds of others. They are all different varieties of the same thing, just bred for different characteristics.

So call it what you like, pepper or chilli, but this is one of those recipes where choosing a big mild chilli pepper over a standard watery one will reap tasty rewards, avoid the mushy stuff and go for some flavour. If you are growing your own, the best flavours come from New Mexico chillies, Italian corno di torro, or even ripe red poblano chillies.

Ingredients

3 large mild red chillies, New Mexico Big Jim or Italian Romano

5 cloves of garlic

1 heaped tbsp fresh basil, chopped

25g grated parmesan

25g pine nuts

3 tbsp extra virgin olive oil

1 tsp salt

1 tsp ground black pepper

Method

- Rub the peppers all over with olive oil using your hands, then place them on a baking tray and roast them for 30-40 minutes in an oven at gas mark 6, 400°F or 200°C. Turn them twice during this time and remove them from the oven when the skins have become uniformly loose. Cover the tray and leave them to cool for 15 minutes or so.

- Whilst the peppers are cooking chop the garlic, basil and pine nuts. You can make things easier by using a blender to mix them with the cheese, oil and seasoning, but I prefer to chop them manually so the end result is a rougher mix, rather than a completely smooth paste. Either way, once chopped or blended, mix all these together in a bowl and move on to dealing with the peppers.

- When the peppers have cooled you should be able to peel off the skins very easily, it can get a bit messy but try and remove all the skins if you can, as they are a bit unpalatable if they find their way into the next stage. You should also remove the seeds from inside. Lay the pepper on a chopping board, pull out the stalk and discard it, slit the pepper lengthways with a knife and open it out flat. Sweep all the seeds out to one side with your fingers.

- The next job is to mix the peppers with the remainder of the ingredients. Again you can use a blender, but the peppers are probably so soft that a light chopping combined with the mixing action will result in a rough paste that makes a delicious ideal pasta sauce.

Harissa

Harissa, a North African paste made predominantly from dried red chillies, and flavoured with caraway seeds and other spices. It is such a versatile ingredient. A little goes a long way, use it to marinade meat, in a sauce for pizza topping, home-made bread, BBQ sauce, the list is endless. It will store for some time, but as this recipe does use some fresh ingredients, keep it refrigerated for up to 2 weeks, or freeze it.

Ingredients

50g dried red chillies (New Mexico or guajillo), seeds and stems removed, or New Mexico chilli powder

1 tbsp fresh coriander, chopped

3 cloves of garlic

1 heaped tsp ground caraway seeds

1 heaped tsp ground cumin

Juice of 1 lime

100ml extra virgin olive oil

½ tsp salt

Method

- If you choose to use dried chillies, remove the seeds and stems, break them into small pieces and grind them in a spice or coffee grinder. They can be quite oily and therefore flexible. You may need to dry them on a tray in a cool oven for a while to make them crunchier and easier to grind.

- Once you have the ingredients together, chop the garlic finely and mix everything thoroughly in a bowl. Store it in a clean jam jar in the fridge.

- There is an easy method of freezing it, take a plastic zip-lock freezer bag and spoon the paste into it, leaving a gap between each spoonful. Lay the bag carefully on a flat surface in the freezer. When you come to use it you can take out one spoonful at a time.

- My favourite easy use of this is to mix a spoonful with yoghurt as a dip. I also mix it with red wine, and a small amount of red wine vinegar as a pork marinade.

- See the later recipe for slow-cooked lamb with harissa.

Berbere Ethiopian Chilli Paste

This blend of dried spices is reminiscent of a Mexican Mole, a complex harissa if you will; an intricate mix of flavours used on grilled meat, and as an addition to lentil dahl, stewed beans or casseroles. You can mix the dried ingredients only and store them for later use, or make up the full recipe for immediate use, or for freezing.

Ingredients

1 tbsp ancho chilli powder

1 tsp ground cumin

1 tsp ground fenugreek

1 tsp ground black pepper

½ tsp turmeric

¼ tsp ground cloves

¼ tsp ground cinnamon

¼ tsp ground nutmeg

1 tsp salt

2cm cube of fresh ginger

3 piri piri chillies (or other bird's-eye chillies)

2 tbsp red wine vinegar

3 cloves of garlic

50ml olive oil

1 tbsp fresh coriander, finely chopped

Method

- Mix the dried spices (ancho, cumin, fenugreek, black pepper, turmeric, cloves, cinnamon, nutmeg and salt) together with the red wine vinegar to make a smooth paste.

- Finely chop the fresh ginger, piri piri chillies, garlic and coriander. Heat the oil gently in a small saucepan, add these freshly chopped ingredients and stir until soft. Do not allow the oil to burn. Remove from the heat and add the paste. Mix until smooth.

- This is a spicy hot paste with intense flavours, use it sparingly to start with, you can always add more.

Dips and Appetizers

CHAPTER 5

Dips and Appetizers

Salsa Macha

I can't think of a recipe with such an unhealthy list of ingredients, and, worse still, it is easy to polish off an awful lot of this stuff in a very short space of time.

But hey-ho, this is an extremely versatile cooking sauce, dip or marinade; akin to satay sauce, but with a spicy and smoky taste. Traditionally it is heavy on chipotles, but I find that using a large proportion of the widely available chipotle morita is too overpoweringly smoky and gives it a burnt flavour. So I usually use less of them, or milder home-smoked chillies, as well as guajillo powder.

Ingredients

150g crunchy peanut butter

3 chipotle moritas (probably more if you have smoked the chillies yourself)

4 cloves of garlic, finely chopped.

100ml olive oil

2 tbsp brown sugar

2 tbsp sherry vinegar or red wine vinegar

2 tsp guajillo chilli powder

1 tsp sesame oil

Method

- This is almost a cheat's recipe, as it uses peanut butter to dispense with the need to blend nuts into the sauce, but this doesn't seem to affect the flavour and it makes the recipe so simple I am more likely to use it.

- Soak the chipotles in a small amount of hot water for about 20 minutes, then take them from the water and chop them finely. Or you can grind them into a powder if you have a spice or coffee grinder.

- In a small saucepan mix all the ingredients together and bring to the boil, simmer for a minute or two whilst stirring constantly. Transfer to a bowl and leave to cool, as it cools the sauce will thicken.

- This is a rich and tasty dip when served with corn chips or pitta breads. It is also a great thing to pour over barbecued meat, as you would chicken satay, but to my mind the extra smoked chilli gives it the edge.

Pimiento de Padron

There is no doubt that these are one of the tastiest and easiest to prepare of all chillies. They are almost unique in that they are picked when still very immature. If left to ripen they grow into a medium sized, much hotter red chilli. They are also very easy to grow, as long as you have plenty of space. As they are picked immature, you can plant seeds in April and have a constant crop by the middle of July. Two plants will give a couple of portions every 5 days in the height of summer.

Spanish tradition says that one in 30 will be a hot one, and eating them can be a bit like Russian roulette. But the occurrence of hotter ones is not completely random, they are simply slightly more mature, the seeds have started to form inside, and so has the heat. If you examine a batch of Padrons, you will observe that most of them are soft with a slightly waxy look and feel to them. Amongst these will be a few that are glossy, possibly bigger, but not always, and if you squeeze one of these you will feel it crunch inside. These are the hotter ones.

Method

- To prepare the padrons, fry them in a hot pan with olive oil.

- Toss them about in the oil until they are coated, and when they start to soften stir them around and press them gently with a spatula to push them into contact with the pan. When they start to blacken they are ready. You can optionally sprinkle them with sea salt before serving. Eat the whole lot, minus the stalks, but watch out for the hot ones.

Guacamole

Commonplace I know, but this is one of the most delicious of all dishes that originate in the new world and one I can't resist.

Ingredients

2 large ripe avocados

100g red onion, chopped (alternatively a mild white Spanish onion)

1 beef tomato (if you use normal tomatoes, remove the pips and juice)

1 large green jalapeño (can be from frozen), an alternative is 3 serranos

2 cloves of garlic

2 limes

1 tbsp fresh coriander, chopped

A few drops of plain habanero sauce (or a small amount of fresh habanero)

Method

• Finely chop the onion, garlic, chilli, coriander and tomato. The consistency of the tomato is important; too much juice and the end product can be too runny. If you can get your hands on a nice meaty beef tomato then do so; if not, and you use normal tomato, remove the squishy juice and seeds before you start chopping.

• Rinse the avocados under a tap; you want them clean so you can use the skins as serving dishes later. Slice the avocados around the middle and remove the stones. Using a spoon, remove all the flesh into a bowl, leaving the skins intact. Squeeze the juice of one of the limes into the bowl. Keep the other one for later.

• Mash the avocado flesh until it is a slightly lumpy paste and mix in all the other ingredients except the second lime.

• Heap the mixture into the four halves of avocado, then squeeze the juice of the second lime over the top, this stops the avocado going brown.

• Serve with tortilla chips, cucumber and courgette sticks, or sliced pitta bread.

Ceviche

Ceviche is a dish of seafood marinated in lime or lemon juice, the acid of the lime juice 'cooks' the flesh of the fish turning it flaky and white. It is probably most commonly associated with Peru, but in fact it is found in coastal regions throughout Central and South America. I have eaten it in the Bahamas, where they use the meat of the conch, and as far south as Chile.

In this recipe I have used gurnard, which for me is a local and sustainable fish, but you can use any firm-fleshed fish such as cod or hake. Freshness of the fish is paramount. Although the fish is 'cooked' in lime juice there is no heat involved so there is still a greater chance of contamination, or that existing bacteria will develop if there are parts of the fish that remain unaffected by the juice. Ceviche is one of my most favourite dishes, and I always think of it first when I see a freshly caught fish, so it is the freshness of the fish, rather than the species which should be at the forefront of your mind when making your choice.

With regard to the chilli, in South America they generally use an aji chilli; these give a sharp citrus-like heat and so are well suited to fish dishes. In tropical Central America you might find ceviche is hotter if they use the habanero chilli, common to that region, and the flavour will be fruitier. You can make this substitution yourself.

Serves 4 as a starter, prepare 4 hours in advance of eating.

Ingredients

200g gurnard fillet or other firm-fleshed fish

2 large spring onions

Juice of 4 limes

1 fresh aji chilli, amarillo, crystal or limon (limon will be hotter)

2 tbsp fresh coriander, chopped

Method

- Remove any bones from the fish and chop into 2 cm cubes so the pieces 'cook' evenly. Chop the spring onions (including the leaves) and the chilli finely. Mix all these ingredients together in a bowl with the coriander and squeeze the lime juice on top. Gently fold everything into the lime juice to avoid breaking up the fish.

- Refrigerate and leave for four hours, turning with a fork half way through. This dish will keep for 24 hours in the refrigerator, but the fish will lose its consistency so it is best eaten fresh.

Warm
Courgette Dip

A tasty dinner party dip, and an easy one to make if you already have the oven on.

Ingredients

300g courgettes

1 large mild red chilli, (poblano, New Mexico or Spanish Pimento will do)

3 cloves of garlic

100ml soured cream

2 tbsp extra virgin olive oil

½ tsp salt

½ tsp ground black pepper

Method

- Cut the courgettes into rough pieces and brush them with some of the oil. Roast the courgette, chilli and the garlic cloves in the oven at gas mark 6, 400°F or 204°C for about 25 minutes.

- Remove from the oven and leave to cool enough for you to remove the chilli skin if it is tough, plus the stem and the seeds from inside. The garlic cloves should slide out from their skins with a single squeeze.

- Add all the ingredients including the remainder of the oil but without the soured cream to a blender and blend until smooth. Stir in the soured cream and serve warm with pitta breads, carrot or courgette sticks.

Salsa Verde with Tomatillos

For the vegetable-grower tomatillos are probably less hassle than any other crop, if you can start them indoors they can be planted into a vegetable patch and will grow prolifically even in temperate climates.

The result is a tomato-like green fruit contained in a husk. They are related to Cape Gooseberries, but are more a vegetable than a fruit and can be stored for months in a cool dark place. They become sweeter when fully ripe but are usually cooked while slightly tart. One plant can be very prolific, but luckily this simple standard recipe is a tasty and healthy way of gobbling them up.

Ingredients

500g tomatillos
(use green tomatoes as a substitute)

100g white onion

100ml water

2 cloves of garlic

1 green jalapeño chilli

1 tbsp fresh oregano, chopped

1 tbsp fresh coriander, chopped

1 tsp salt

Method

- Pre-heat your oven to gas mark 6, 400°F or 204°C. Put the tomatillos, the onion, the garlic cloves and the chilli into a greased baking tray and roast in the oven for 20 minutes.

- Remove from the oven, remove the husk from the garlic cloves, the outer skins of the onion and the stem from the chilli, chop everything into chunks and transfer to a saucepan with the oregano, coriander, some of the water and the salt. Simmer and stir until the chunks start to break down. When they have become mostly liquid transfer to a blender, or use a stick blender, to reduce them to a sauce. Add a little more of the water if necessary. You are aiming for something that can be scooped, rather than a runny sauce. Tomatillos can be a little hit and miss in terms of their ripeness, if the sauce is a little too sharp, then a teaspoon if sugar might help.

- Us this as an accompaniment to roasted meat, as you would use apple sauce with pork. You can serve it on its own as a dip with corn chips and pitta bread, or you can use it as a cooking sauce to garnish enchiladas. If you serve it as a dip on its own try stirring in a dollop of soured cream.

Spicy Squash Soup

A warming and filling winter soup, the ancho powder gives a great depth of flavour without making this too hot.

Ingredients

1 large or two small butternut squash (about 1kg of flesh)

150g white onion, chopped

500ml water

200ml double cream

100g carrots, grated

25g salted butter

1 clove of garlic, chopped

10g ancho powder

1 vegetable stock cube

1 tbsp olive oil

½ tsp cumin powder

½ tsp salt

Method

- In a large saucepan, soften the onions, garlic and carrot in the butter and oil. Cut the flesh of the squash into small cubes and when the onions have softened, add the squash, water, stock cube, ancho powder, cumin and salt. Bring to the boil and simmer for about 30 minutes. Transfer to a blender and blend until smooth, alternatively use a stick blender directly into the pan. Transfer back into the pan if need be, add the cream and bring back to a simmer before serving.

Refried Bean Soup

I often used tinned refried beans, but if you make them yourself using tinned beans it isn't much extra work and you can vary the flavours if you like with different beans, more onion, or a variety of spices.

The name refried beans is confusing, it is derived from the Spanish word 'refritos' which means 'well-fried' not 'fried for a second time'. This makes the recipe even simpler than it sounds; there will be no re-frying of beans here.

This recipe will make enough for two generous and filling servings, double things up for four.

For the Refried Beans

400g pinto or cannellini beans

1 spring onion, finely chopped

3 tbsp olive oil

1 tsp cumin powder

1 tsp guajillo powder

½ tsp salt

½ tsp black pepper

- In a small saucepan soften the spring onion in the oil and add the drained beans and spices. Keep stirring and mashing the beans until they are mostly broken down and smooth. That's it for the beans; these can now be used in this recipe or any other.

For the Soup

- You can go straight from the beans to the soup in the same pan if you like, though you will need to fry some onion separately first.

Refried beans as above (or a 400g tin)

400ml water

100g skinned green chilli, Anaheim or New Mexico (or chopped green pepper)

75g Cheddar cheese

50g white onion, chopped

1 chicken stock cube

Oil for frying

- Soften the onion in the oil first, chop the chilli into pieces, then combine all the ingredients together in a saucepan and bring to the boil. When the cheese has melted and the chilli has softened you need to blend the soup, either in a separate blender or with a stick blender.

Grapefruit and Chilli Salad

Do not be deceived by the simplicity of this recipe, it sounds a little off-the-wall but it is a refreshing sweet and sour accompaniment to barbecued meat, oily fish or roast pork. Be careful to chop the habanero as finely as you can, even crushing the pieces with the side of a knife to reduce it to a pulp. It has quite a direct searing heat, but one which doesn't seem to linger. Earlier in the book I described how you can preserve chillies in honey, and I always keep a few habaneros that way. Chillies preserved in honey make this recipe even easier to prepare.

Ingredients

2 grapefruits, segmented and skinned (a tin is ok, provided it is unsweetened, but fresh is more firm)

1 spring onion, finely chopped

2 tbsp honey

2 tbsp white wine vinegar

½ fresh habanero chilli

Method

- There are various ways of removing the fleshy middle from grapefruit segments. I find that rather than peeling it as you would an orange, the best way is to cut off the top and bottom so it sits flat on a chopping board, then remove the peel by slicing downwards round the edges but cutting deeper than just the outer peel so you remove the pith and the outside skin of the segments at the same time. Work your way around the grapefruit until you are left with a roughly round ball of exposed flesh. Then you can run your knife down the insides of each segment and the fleshy segments should just fall out.

- Place the grapefruit segments in a small serving dish. Mix together all the other ingredients in a bowl and pour them over the grapefruit half an hour before serving to allow the flavours to mingle.

Sweet Thai Cucumber Salad

I find it is most often the case that when a dish is placed before you, the spiciness usually comes from the main, often meaty centrepiece, and any accompanying vegetable matter is there to tone it down. This quick and fragrant salad is quite the opposite. Although it can provide a moist and refreshing contrast to something that is less so, it carries with it a spicy zest. This goes very well with the courgette fritter recipe featured later in this book.

Ingredients

½ cucumber, thinly sliced

1 spring onion, finely chopped

Juice of ½ a lime

3 hot Thai chillies, finely chopped (use 'Twilight' or any small bird's-eye chillies as an alternative)

1 tbsp olive oil

1 tbsp rice wine vinegar

1 tbsp fish sauce

1 tbsp honey

1 inch lemon grass stem, finely chopped

½ tbsp fresh coriander, chopped

½ tsp salt

Method

- Mix the dressing first by chopping the chillies, lemon grass and coriander, then combining them with the olive oil, vinegar, fish sauce, honey, lime juice and salt.

- Toss together the chopped spring onion and cucumber, then mix in the dressing.

Stuffed Chilaca Chillies with Avocado Cream

Chilaca is the fresh chilli variety from which we get the dried pasilla. I have always grown them for drying, but a friend who spent their youth in Mexico told me about eating them stuffed with cheese. These will appeal to fans of pimiento de padron, a similar but slightly stronger taste. You can also use poblanos for this recipe.

One of these per person is enough for a small snack or starter.

Ingredients

4 chilaca chillies

40g Cheddar cheese

2 cloves of garlic

100ml soured cream

1 small avocado

Oil for frying

Method

- Grill and skin the chillies as described earlier. Leaving the stalks in place, slice them open lengthways and remove the seeds with a teaspoon. Place pieces of the cheese inside, along their whole length.

- Remove the flesh from the avocado and add it with the soured cream to a blender ready for mixing.

- Lay the chillies in a frying pan with a little oil, and also add the cloves of garlic, still with their skins on. Fry the chillies for about a minute on each side. If the cheese starts to escape, don't worry, fried cheese tastes even better than melted. Toss the garlic cloves around in the oil too and they will soon soften.

- Put the chillies on their plates and remove the garlic from its skins, the clove inside should have softened enough to just slip out. Add the cloves to the blender with the avocado and cream. Blend until smooth and serve over the chillies.

Chilli Paneer

An easy to prepare side dish or a tasty vegetarian meal; this is best served immediately after cooking whilst the paneer pieces are still crispy on the outside and soft in the middle.

I have discovered there are two types of chilli paneer, the one I cook, which is known as dry paneer, and another version with a sauce, usually referred to as paneer with gravy. You can buy paneer in supermarkets; it is an Indian cheese, slightly rubbery in texture which holds together without melting when cooked. Halloumi is roughly the same, I believe they are both of Middle Eastern origin and you can make this recipe with halloumi if you like.

Ingredients

250g paneer cheese	1 tbsp soy sauce
1 green pepper, sliced and seeds removed	1 tbsp red wine vinegar
50g onion, chopped	1 tbsp tomato purée
25g cornflour	3 cloves of garlic
1 fresh red Hungarian Wax chilli	1 spring onion, chopped
10g Kashmiri chilli powder	1 cm cube fresh ginger, chopped
3 tbsp sunflower oil (or similar) for frying	½ tsp salt

Method

- Mix the cornflour, Kashmiri chilli powder and salt together in a bowl, and cut the paneer into 2cm cubes. Toss the cubes in the flour mix to evenly coat them then fry them in a wok or small frying pan using the cooking oil. Make sure they are evenly fried until they start to turn golden but don't mess with them so much that they start to break down.

- Remove the paneer pieces from the pan; most of the oil will have soaked into the flour. In the same pan or wok quickly fry the sliced pepper, chopped onion, red chilli, garlic, and ginger along with the soy sauce, vinegar and tomato purée.

- When the pepper and onion start to soften, but while still retaining their shape and a little crispness, turn off the heat and stir in the paneer pieces and the chopped spring onion.

Main Dishes

CHAPTER 6

Main Dishes

Poblano Chilli Rellenos

This is a revered Mexican dish which really illustrates how the poblano chilli stands above sweet peppers or other mild chilli when stuffed and roasted. The flesh is firm, almost leathery, and doesn't break down into a mush when baked. It has a slight chilli heat and a much more concentrated flavour than a standard sweet pepper. In the past I have roasted them side by side to illustrate this point. I guarantee that once you have worked with poblano chillies, nothing else will do.

You do need to remove the skins using one of the methods mentioned earlier. Once you have done so you can carefully make a T-shaped opening on the side near the top to remove the seeds. With a sharp knife cut through the tough piece inside the chilli beneath where the stem joins, you can then remove most of the seeds in one go. Scrape the others out with a spoon; they are definitely unpalatable if they find their way onto your plate. Fill the chilli with a stuffing of your choice, a beef picadillo is more traditional, but later in the book is a Mexican turkey picadillo recipe, which is my favourite. Alternatively a vegetarian risotto or flavoured beans will do the trick. Try not to make the filling too spicy, you don't want to overshadow the flavour of the poblano.

When stuffed with a warm filling they should be roasted on a baking tray, topped with cheese and covered with foil for 20 minutes at gas mark 6, 400°F or 200°C. Serve them alongside refried beans and rice.

Rajas Burrito

This is a simple dish comprising strips of poblano or New Mexico green chillies with a soured cream sauce. It is usually quite mild and quick to prepare, providing you are skilled in skinning your chillies first.

Eat it as a lunchtime snack or an evening appetiser. I'd like to say you can use sweet peppers as a substitute, but really this is a dish based around the distinctive flavours of slow-grown green chillies and a sweet pepper simply isn't going to have that edge, so reserve this recipe for the time when you have grown, or can get your hands on the real thing.

Ingredients

6 green poblano or New Mexico chillies (Anaheim, New Mexico 6-4 or 'Joe E Parker' will be mildest, poblano and sandia a bit hotter)

200ml soured cream

125g white onion, chopped

25g grated Cheddar cheese

1 tsp dried oregano

salt

pepper

Method

- Start by skinning your chillies as described earlier. Once you have done so, remove the stems and the seeds from inside, and cut them into 1cm wide strips.

- Heat some oil in a pan and soften the chopped onion. Add the strips, toss in with the onion then add the soured cream, the cheese, oregano and a little salt and pepper. Simmer the mixture for a minute or two whilst you fold the strips into the sauce. The green colour of the chillies should leach out into the sauce as it thickens.

- Leave the mixture to cool for a few minutes and the sauce will thicken more. Serve wrapped in a warm corn tortilla.

- The cheese shouldn't overpower this dish, it is all about the roasted chilli taste but as an alternative to this recipe you can uses blue cheese for a tangier flavour.

Green Chilli and Green Bean Salad

The thick flesh of the chillies, the filling beans and the avocado, together with a mouth-watering dressing, make this not just a side salad, but a hearty meal that stands on its own merits. Serve it while the beans and chillies are still slightly warm from steaming for the best flavours.

Ingredients

250g fresh dwarf French beans

3 large green chillies (New Mexico, Anaheim or romano peppers)

1 avocado

1 large beef tomato, chopped

50g parmesan cheese, grated or crumbled

2 spring onions, finely chopped

1 small jalapeño chilli, finely chopped

2 tbsp extra virgin olive oil

2 tbsp white wine vinegar

1 tbsp fresh coriander, chopped

Juice of ½ a lime

1 tsp dried oregano

½ tsp salt

Method

- Grill the green chillies and remove the skins, stems and the seeds inside.

- Prepare the dressing in a small bowl using the vinegar, oil, coriander, oregano and salt. Add the finely chopped spring onions and jalapeño.

- Steam the beans until they start to go limp, normally around 4-6 minutes depending on how big they are. Cut the chillies into strips and just at the point the beans are starting to bend easily add the pepper strips and steam for another minute. Be careful not to steam the beans to the point where they start to lose their dark green colour and go pale. Transfer them to a serving bowl and leave to cool for a few minutes while you chop the avocado and tomato.

- When the beans and chilli strips have stopped steaming, but while still slightly warm, stir in the parmesan, followed by the avocado and tomato, and finally the dressing.

Caribbean Brown Chicken Stew

Although this has a fairly uninspiring name it is a really worthwhile dish to perfect. It has the flavours of jerk chicken; the thyme and allspice, but rather than being a dry marinade for grilled or barbecued meat, it is a saucy stew.

The presence of soy sauce may seem out of place but it is common in Jamaican cooking. You can do all the cooking in one pan if you have something broad enough to fry the chicken first and deep enough to hold the liquid. There is no limit to how hot you can make this one; the allspice and thyme are robust enough flavours to come through even if you double the chilli content so feel free to experiment.

Ingredients

750g chicken pieces (thighs, legs or quarters)
Approximately 400ml water
150g onion, roughly chopped
150g sliced carrots
2 spring onions, chopped
3 cloves of garlic
Juice of 1 lime
2 habanero / scotch bonnet chillies
3 tbsp soy sauce
1 tbsp fresh thyme leaves
2 tsp ground allspice
2cm cube of fresh ginger, chopped
3 tsp cornflour
1 tsp ground black pepper
1 tsp salt
Oil for frying

Method

- You will need to prepare the marinade in advanced of cooking.

- Add together the lime juice, soy sauce, garlic, ginger, chopped chilies, thyme, allspice, salt and pepper to make a marinade. You can mix them in a blender, but I prefer the slightly rough appearance of the chopped chilli and garlic. Rub this all over the chicken pieces and leave them refrigerated, preferably overnight to allow the meat to marinade.

- Brown the chicken pieces in a frying pan with a little oil. Mix the cornflour into the remaining marinade and add everything to a deep pan along with the carrots, onion and water. Simmer for 30-40 minutes or until the chicken is cooked through and easily separated from the bone when you poke it with a knife. You can adjust the thickness of the sauce with extra cornflour or water if need be. Finally, stir in the spring onions for a bit of colour and serve over rice.

Courgette Fritters

This is a great way to enjoy some fairly mild chillies, such as Hungarian wax or 'Inferno'. You can use anything that is fleshy, preferably with a mild amount of heat. Wax chillies won't need to be skinned, but if you choose something bigger you will probably have to grill and skin them first.

This recipe is enough to make around 8 fritters.

Ingredients

250g courgettes	50g parmesan cheese
100g mild wax chilli, seeds and stems removed	1 tbsp fresh coriander, chopped
100g finely sliced red onion	1 tbsp olive oil
100g plain flour	½ tsp salt
2 eggs	½ tsp ground black pepper

Method

- Grate the courgette and cut the chillies into fine strips. The chillies will need to be partly cooked, so lay them under a grill for a few minutes first; this will be your opportunity to remove the skins if they are tough.

- Mix the egg, flour, oil, salt and pepper in a large mixing bowl then add in the courgette, chillies, onion, parmesan cheese and coriander. Gently mix everything together until the vegetables are nicely coated. This will still be a fairly runny mixture and if left the liquid will settle to the bottom of the bowl.

- Heat a non-stick frying pan with a little oil. Form roughly heaped tablespoons of the mix and dollop them into the pan, roughly form them into even shapes with the spoon as they start to fry. Do not be tempted to flip them over for the first couple of minutes or they will fall apart. After this time they should come free of the pan if you try and push them around with a spatula. Flip them over for another couple of minutes, then reduce the heat to a minimum to stop them burning and cook for another 8 minutes or so, or until they are cooked through.

- I think these are a meal on their own, and like to serve them with just a dollop of mango chutney and a small salad, maybe the 'Thai Cucumber Salad' listed earlier.

Barbecued Pork Ribs

Although the elapsed time it takes to prepare this meal is great, most of it is waiting time, other than that it is a surprisingly easy and rewarding meal.

The Barbecue Sauce

100ml white wine vinegar

200ml water

100g tomato purée

4 tbsp honey

2 cloves of garlic, chopped

4 tsp New Mexico red chilli powder

1 chipotle chilli (either reconstituted from dry, or in adobo sauce)

2 tsp achiote paste or annatto powder

2 tbsp Worcester sauce

2 tsp English mustard

2 bay leaves

1 tsp salt

- Combine all the ingredients in a small pan and simmer for a few minutes, while stirring to make sure it doesn't burn. When things have combined nicely, leave the sauce for half an hour while the bay leaves infuse. When it has cooled slightly, it is easier to rub into the ribs.

The Ribs

- This recipe uses baby back ribs, the meatier cut from the top of the pig, rather than the belly side spare ribs, which carry less meat and more fat. You will need 2kg of ribs; this should be enough to feed four. Prepare them by removing, if you can, the thin membrane that covers the inside of the ribs, this is a tough layer that you don't need, and inhibits the flavours from penetrating the meat.

- Smother the ribs with about 1/3rd of the sauce and leave in the refrigerator for a few hours, or overnight. Be careful not to contaminate the remaining sauce with raw pork juices.

- About 4 hours ahead of eating, put the ribs on a wire tray in a roasting tin, and cover with aluminium foil. Bake them in the oven at about gas mark 1.5, 284°F or 140°C for 3 hours. This low temperature and length of cooking time is essential to tenderise the meat and break down the chewy bits into tasty bits. Nothing should burn at this stage, ovens vary, and at these low temperatures a small variation can make all the difference, so check them every once in a while. They should be hot and dripping slowly but not sizzling. If anything looks burnt, turn down the heat, and if it the meat looks like it is drying out, baste them a little with the juices and turn down the heat slightly.

- After 3 hours, remove them, coat them thoroughly with most of the remaining sauce, and return them to the oven, uncovered, this time at gas mark 6 or 400°F or 200°C for around 20 minutes, a bit longer if you want them crispy.

- Keep a little of the sauce back for a final coating as you serve.

Chilli Con Carne

With Kidney Beans - A Very British Dish?

This is another one of my favourite recipes and one which has grown with me for 25 years. I am sure it has evolved over those years, but this is the recipe I keep to now.

Serves 6

There is a range of chillies in this one, I think the individual flavours are vital to give it lots of depth, the fresh chillies bring something, and the dried ones bring something else.

I have always believed the myth that using kidney beans in a chilli is peculiar to Britain and that in Mexico and the USA they find this a little weird, preferring to use black beans, pinto beans, or even no beans at all. Recently though, I was browsing a Tex-Mex cookery book published in California in 1969, and it recommended kidney beans. So there you go, not exclusively British after all.

Manteca de Cerdo is Mexican lard (lard is from pork, dripping is from beef) and it has something extra over the lard you buy in shops as it isn't pure, it has meaty flavours too. There are details on how to make your own earlier in this book.

Ingredients

500g lean minced beef	1 chicken stock cube
150g red onion, chopped	1 chipotle chilli
400g tin kidney beans	1 dried ancho chilli (or 1 tbsp ancho powder)
400g tin plum tomatoes	1 dried New Mexico chilli
1 glass (125ml) red wine	1 tbsp fresh coriander, chopped
1 beef tomato (or two large tomatoes)	1 tbsp fresh oregano (or 1 tsp dried)
2 tbsp tomato purée	2 tsp ground cumin
1 tbsp manteca de cerdo (rendered pork fat, use lard as a substitute)	2 bay leaves
3 cloves of garlic, chopped	15g chocolate (as dark as you can get)
1 fresh green jalapeño, chopped	1 tsp ground black pepper
1 fresh habanero chopped	1 tsp salt

Method

- Tear up the ancho, chipotle, and New Mexico chillies into a small bowl of hot water to rehydrate them. In a large pan, soften the onion and garlic in the oil, then brown off the mince. Add the manteca (or lard), the chicken stock, cumin, bay leaves, red wine, tomato purée, jalapeño, chocolate, habanero, salt and pepper. Blend the rehydrated chillies in their water until smooth (or finely chop them) and add those too. Continue to simmer as you add the tin of tomatoes and the beans.

- All the ingredients, with the exception of the fresh tomato, the coriander, and the oregano are now bubbling away together. If it starts to burn or becomes too dry add a little water or more wine. The longer you can leave this the more the flavour infuses, but it will need regular stirring. Alternatively you can keep it refrigerated overnight and reheat it. Just before serving roughly chop the fresh tomato and the fresh herbs and add those in.

- Serve with rice, soured cream and avocado.

Mexican Picadillo, with Turkey and Courgette

Picadillo is most often made with minced beef, but I make it all the time with turkey, which is flavoursome, cheap and healthy. The resulting picadillo is served with rice, in tacos, or as a stuffing for poblano chillies.

Ingredients

500g minced turkey

200g finely chopped courgette

125g red onion, chopped

1 fresh green jalapeño chilli

2 large tomatoes

2 tbsp tomato purée

2 cloves of garlic, chopped

1 tbsp chopped fresh oregano (alternatively, marjoram or dried oregano)

1 tbsp fresh parsley, chopped

1 tbsp ancho powder

1 bay leaf

1 chicken stock cube

½ tsp salt

½ tsp ground black pepper

Method

• Soften the onions and garlic in a shallow pan before adding the minced turkey. Fry off the turkey and add all the other ingredients except the parsley which you should add just before serving. If you are using picadillo to stuff chillies or peppers this should make enough for at least half a dozen large ones, if not 8.

Slow-Cooked Lamb with Harissa

This is comfort food at its best. It has characteristics of lamb tagine, and is hugely flavoursome considering its simplicity and ease of preparation. It needs a few minutes preparation in advance, but as a slow cook recipe it provides a hearty reward after a long winter walk at just the time when you need instant gratification. I normally use shoulder fillets, fairly tough but lean cuts of meat. You can use any cut of lamb, but try and remove most of the fat before cooking or the resulting sauce will be too oily.

Ingredients

500g lamb shoulder fillet

200g mushrooms

200ml port

200ml boiled water

2 tbsp harissa paste

Method

- Preheat your oven to gas mark 3, 325°F, 170°C

- Boil a kettle of water. Cut the lamb into 3cm chunks and place into a small, lidded casserole dish. Add the port, aproximately 200ml of hot water, or enough to make sure the chunks are well covered, and the harissa paste.

- Place in the middle of your oven and cook for 30 minutes, at this point you can check to make sure it is bubbling nicely. If so turn your oven down to gas mark 1, 275°F, 140°C and leave for a further two hours. You can check periodically that the liquid hasn't boiled dry, if so add some more water, but it really shouldn't have thickened at all unless your oven tends towards the hot side. After the two hours are up, slice in the mushrooms and return to the oven for a further 30 minutes.

- Serve with rice or couscous. At the end, the sauce should be quite liquid and soak into the rice.

Aji de Gallina

A traditional Peruvian dish using aji amarillo, a fairly mild chilli with a herby citrus taste. Gallina is a Spanish word for hen, I have no idea why the dish uses this word rather than 'pollo', the word for chicken, just tradition I think.

Serves 6

The sauce is creamy and you could look upon this as a South American Chicken Korma. This is a very filling dish, the sauce in itself is wholesome, with lots of nuts and bread, and with the eggs too it makes for quite a heavy meal, something for the starving hungry on a cold day. Serve it with white rice or as an alternative use another Peruvian tradition, potatoes, maybe some nice waxy new potatoes, but don't go overboard on the accompaniment, this is almost a meal in itself.

Ingredients

500g chicken breasts

600ml water

150g onion, roughly chopped

1 200ml tin of evaporated milk

75g chopped walnuts

75g slightly stale bread (ideally from a crusty loaf, not sliced bread).

3 hard-boiled eggs

5 aji amarillo chillies (can be fresh, frozen or reconstituted from dried)

50g grated Parmesan cheese

3 cloves of garlic

1 tbsp olive oil

1 tsp achiote paste or ½ tsp turmeric

1 tsp salt

Method

- Cut the chicken breast in two down their length and boil them for around 20 minutes in 500ml of water with the salt.

- If you are using dried aji chillies rather than fresh, rehydrate them now by soaking them in hot water for 20 minutes.

- Peel and crush the garlic cloves and add these, along with the chopped onion to the boiling chicken.

- If you don't have hard boiled eggs to hand, you can boil them now, do it in a separate pan to the chicken in case you break one. Put them in a pan of cool water, bring them to the boil and continue to boil for 7 minutes. Remove them from the water and let them cool before peeling them.

- After 20 minutes fish out the chicken and put it aside, do not throw away the stock and onions, this will be the base for your sauce.

- If you are using fresh amarillo chillies slice them open and take out the seeds which means removing the internal strips to which they are attached, this will remove some of the heat. Leave the seeds in if you like but don't overdo it, that's not the idea of this dish.

- Pulp the walnuts in a blender with the onion stock. Add the bread, evaporated milk, olive oil and achiote paste (or turmeric). Blend them all until they form a fairly smooth sauce. You can do this job using a stick blender in the pan if you wish.

- Shred or chop the chicken roughly, then combine it, and the Parmesan cheese with the sauce. Simmer and stir. The sauce should have the consistency of a thick soup, if it is already too thick, add a little water.

- Peel the hard boiled eggs, and slice them into quarters. Take the sauce from the heat and stir in the egg pieces at the last minute.

Goan Fish Curry

This is a very quick dish to prepare, provided you have fish already filleted. I have used bream and bass for this recipe, but the choice is yours. The Kashmiri chillies make this a mild dish, but still impart a lot of flavour.

Ingredients

400g firm fish fillets
(preferably with the skin still on)

400ml tin of coconut milk

200g chopped ripe tomatoes (or tinned)

2 tomatoes, roughly chopped (keep until last)

150g white onion, chopped

8 dried Kashmiri chillies

2 red jalapeño or serrano chillies

2 tbsp olive oil

1 tbsp fresh coriander, chopped

2 tbsp tamarind paste

3 cloves of garlic, chopped

1 tsp cumin powder

1 tsp fenugreek powder

½ tsp turmeric

1cm cube fresh ginger, chopped

½ tsp sugar

salt

Method

- Break up the Kashmiri chillies and rehydrate them in hot water, alternatively powder them in a spice grinder. Soften the onions, garlic, jalapeño and ginger in a saucepan with the oil. After a few minutes, add the first lot of tomatoes, the cumin, fenugreek, tamarind paste, turmeric, sugar and salt. Then stir in the coconut milk and bring to the boil. After simmering for a couple of minutes, blend to a saucy consistency and return to the pan. Cut your fish fillets into 3, with the skin still on, and add them to the sauce along with the remaining chunks of tomato and the coriander. Simmer for 5 minutes, maybe longer if you are using another kind of fish with chunkier fillets. Without breaking the fillets apart, check that the fish will flake, and is therefore cooked through. Serve with boiled rice.

Spicy Rice

This is a regular dish in our household, not quite a meal in itself, but substantial enough that it can become one with the addition of a couple of fried eggs and some hot sauce. Alternatively it is a great start for stuffing Spanish pimentos or Mexican poblanos, or as an accompaniment to meat dishes.

Ingredients

200g basmati rice

100g red onion, chopped

100g courgette, chopped

100ml red wine

2 chopped yellow Hungarian Wax chillies

2 spring onions, chopped

2 cloves of garlic chopped

1 tbsp olive oil

1 tbsp tomato purée

1 chopped jalapeño chilli

1 tbsp fresh coriander, chopped

1 tsp achiote paste or ½ tsp turmeric

1 tsp dried oregano

1 bay leaf

Method

- Soften the onion and garlic with the oil in a frying pan, add the chopped courgette, chopped wax chillies, jalapeño chilli, oregano, tomato purée, bay leaf and red wine. Cook slowly for a few minutes whilst you prepare the rice, then turn off the heat.

- Boil 200g of basmati rice with some salt using the achiote paste or turmeric to colour it. Once cooked, drain and leave to cool for a few minutes before adding to the pan; too soon and it will go stodgy.

- Add the rice, chopped spring onions, including the green parts and the coriander to the pan and stir everything together before serving.

Salpicon

Salpicon is a light meat salad served cool, and can be eaten on its own or as a burrito or taco filling. You can use any meat, but chicken is the easiest to prepare and makes for a light option that goes well in tacos.

Serves 4

There are three stages to the recipe, the boiling of the meat, the preparation of the vinaigrette dressing and the chopping of the salad vegetables. All three are combined before serving. This is a crisp fresh dish and you should use a chilli to complement this, fresh aji are ideal, but you can use other fairly hot alternatives such as Bulgarian carrot, Cheyenne, or serrano.

This recipe makes enough for 8 small tacos, which should be a lunch for four people.

Ingredients

400g chicken breast

1 large avocado

1 large beef tomato

50g red onion, very thinly sliced

½ cucumber, julienned or sliced into thin strips

1 tbsp fresh coriander, chopped

2 aji limon chillies, finely chopped (alternatively, aji crystal, or something fresh and zesty, Bulgarian carrot or 'Cheyenne')

Juice of 1 lime

3 tbsp red wine vinegar

2 tbsp extra virgin olive oil

2 tsp dried oregano

1 bay leaf

½ tsp salt

½ tsp ground black pepper

Method

- Slice each chicken breast lengthwise into four strips; add to a saucepan of salted boiling water with the bay leaf. Simmer them for about 8 minutes, then drain and discard the bay leaf.

- Mix the dressing using the oil, lime juice, chopped chilli, vinegar, oregano, salt and pepper.

- Chop the avocado and tomato into small cubes and mix with the cucumber strips, the onion and the chopped coriander.

- When the chicken has cooled slightly, tear it into small pieces. Mix this evenly with the dressing and then fold in the salad. The result should be served immediately at room temperature in warm taco shells.

Enchiladas

This is such a regular favourite in our house that I don't even know where the recipe came from, or whether it is authentic or not. Enchiladas are a wholesome filling dish, so popular that there are as many variations as there are people that cook it.

I use a lot of green stuff, beans, parsley, green jalapeños, I think these offset the heaviness of the cheese and refried beans a little. I tend to use flour tortillas for this. You can use corn tortillas if you wish, but they are generally smaller and don't hold their filling as well when rolled up. I have suggested using beef tomatoes for this recipe, I grow a lot of them, ones that don't go watery but jut dissolve into a thick sauce. Given a choice, I would use them in preference to tinned tomatoes. However I don't want to impose any pompousness on people, tinned plum tomatoes are often a better alternative to fresh, shop bought ones, and I often find myself making this choice.

Allowing two enchiladas per person,
this makes a generous meal for four.

Ingredients

500g minced beef

400g large beef tomatoes (alternatively use a tin
of plum tomatoes)

100g small French beans

400g tin refried beans

150g red onion, chopped

150ml red wine

50ml olive oil

3 cloves of garlic

3 tbsp tomato purée

3 jalapeño chillies (retain 1 for decoration)

1 tbsp fresh parsley, chopped

1 tbsp fresh coriander, chopped

1 chicken stock cube

2 chipotle in adobo sauce (or 2 chipotle chilli,
rehydrated and chopped)

2 tsp hot New Mexico chilli powder

¼ fresh habanero chilli or 1 tsp habanero sauce

1 tsp cumin powder

1 tsp pasilla chilli powder

½ tsp ground black pepper

½ tsp salt

Method

- Preheat your oven to gas mark 6, 400°F or 204°C

- Retain 50ml of the wine, 25ml of the oil and 1 tablespoon of the tomato purée in a bowl to make a garnishing sauce at the end.

- Soften the onions and garlic in the pan with some of the olive oil. When soft, add the mince and fry until browned. Add in the stock cube, most of the tomato purée, the chopped tomatoes, chipotles, all the spices, the seasoning, most of the red wine and two of the chopped jalapeños. Simmer until the liquid starts to reduce and then add the chopped green beans, the parsley and the coriander.

- Grease a large baking dish with olive oil. Lay out the tortillas on a flat plate and make a 'plug' of refried beans at either side of the first one so that when you roll them up the sauce doesn't escape out of the ends. Making sure you have a couple of spoons of sauce left in the pan at the end, spoon in some of the sauce and fold over one side of the tortilla then the other. Repeat for the other 7 tortillas, laying each into the baking dish alongside each other.

- Returning to the pan, use the remaining wine, oil and tomato purée to mix with the last of the sauce and deglaze the pan. A minute of stirring on low heat should do it. Use this liquid to spread over the tops of the folded enchiladas in the dish, try and work it between them a little to stop them sticking together.

- Sprinkle the cheese on top, and garnish with sliced jalapeño and tomato. Cover with tin foil for the first 15 minutes of baking, and then remove it to brown the top slightly for the last 5 minutes.

- Serve with rice accompanied by a tomato, onion and coriander salsa.

Piri Piri Chicken

Piri piri, pili pili and peri peri are names of African origin that apply to small bird's-eye chillies introduced to Africa by Portuguese traders. The names cover a whole host of tiny red chillies that grow all over Southern Africa and at some point they were introduced into Portugal, this is where my own stocks come from.

My mother keeps a plant grown from seed she gathered in Portugal, it is 12 years old and the only chilli plant she grows, so the seeds are never cross pollinated. I call it the mother plant and every year I get fresh seeds from it.

They are pretty hot, probably around 80,000 SHU, so you don't need many to spice up a few bits of chicken, therefore you will need something else to add a bit of extra chilli colour and flavour, hence the ancho powder.

Ingredients

1kg chicken thighs	1 tbsp plain flour
6 piri piri chillies, chopped (or small hot bird's-eye chillies)	1 tbsp fresh parsley, chopped
	1 tbsp red wine vinegar
4 cloves of garlic, chopped	2 tbsp olive oil
Juice of 1 lime	1 tsp dried oregano
1 tbsp ancho powder	1 tsp salt

Method

- Preheat your oven to Gas Mark 4, 350°F, 180°C.

- Mix all the ingredients, apart from the chicken, together in a bowl. The piri piri provides the heat, the ancho provides depth of flavour, and the lime and vinegar give a zesty sharpness. They should form a thick brown mush.

- Smear this thick marinade all over the chicken. Use a spoon rather than your fingers to rub it over and under the skin as the piri piri make it is quite a potent mix. Leave to stand in the refrigerator for at least a couple of hours, if not overnight.

- Place the chicken pieces in a roasting tray and cook them in the oven for around 50 minutes. The tops should brown but not burn; test them to make sure they are cooked through by piercing with a knife.

Desserts and Sweet Things

CHAPTER 7

Desserts and Sweet Things

Chilli Chocolate

Making chilli chocolate may seem a tricky process until you have done it a couple of times, then it will become second nature. You will be glad to hear that working with a large quantity of chocolate makes everything easier than if you just do it 100g at a time, so prepare to make a month's worth in one go, whatever a month's worth is!

In order to make the resulting chocolate shiny and crisp it needs to be tempered. Tempering is a process whereby the chocolate is melted and set at critical temperatures in order to ensure it crystallises, rather than setting into something soft, dull and liable to develop a white bloom. Chocolate can be tempered over and over again, and the beauty of that is you can have another go if you don't get it right first time. You won't overcook it, it doesn't evaporate and you can also use leftovers and scrapings in the next batch. Be careful, however, to avoid any moisture getting into the melted chocolate, this will ruin the

process instantly and the end result, whilst perfectly edible and just as tasty, will not have the desired texture and appearance. Un-tempered chocolate, set at the wrong temperature, will be softer and dull to look at, and will also develop a white bloom.

Because adding moisture to chocolate will ruin the tempering process you cannot use fresh chillies in chocolate, you must use powder. Use fine chilli powder, and something hot that doesn't need to be used in such a large quantity that it makes the chocolate gritty. You can buy chilli oil from suppliers of chocolate making ingredients, but this will give heat but no flavour, so you should select a chilli that gives something extra. My favourite flavours are the aji chillies and habaneros. There is nothing to be lost and everything to be gained by blending different types until you find your preferred mix. If you use an aji then you will want to use the hotter lemon chillies, so aji limon, limo, or lemon drop will do the trick.

Ingredients

200g chocolate (60-70% cocoa is my preferred strength for chilli chocolate, but you can use milk or white if you like)

2g hot chilli powder

Method

- You will need approximately 1g of chilli powder for every 100g of chocolate. The quantity can vary depending on what chilli you use, and what your needs are in terms of heat. This quantity won't blow your head off, but should give enough heat for most people's tastes. For best results you will also need a food thermometer, you can follow this guide without one and your results may be satisfactory, but the chances are you won't succeed in tempering properly.

- You will need a saucepan, and a bowl which sits nicely in the top of the saucepan without touching the bottom, a flexible spatula, and either chocolate moulds or something cool which you can cover with grease proof paper to lay out your chocolate; a marble pastry board, or maybe just the kitchen work surface will do. If the bowl is made from flexible plastic, this will help later on with removing the set remains from around the inside.

- Boil some water in the pan, enough so that the bowl will just touch the water.

- Break up the chocolate and then chop it into finer pieces with a knife.

- Retaining ¼ of the chocolate for later, put ¾ into the bowl and sit it over the saucepan of hot water. The inside of the bowl should be completely free of moisture and at this point the water should not be boiling, turn off the heat.

- Add in the chili powder and stir the chocolate as it melts over the warm water. Use the thermometer to read the temperature, it should reach approximately 120°F, 49°C for dark chocolate, and 110°F, 43°C for milk chocolate. Do not let it go more than a couple of degrees above these temperatures.

- At this point replace the water in the pan with cold tap water, always being careful not to get water in the chocolate.

- Mix in the remaining ¼ of the chocolate to help reduce the temperature, stirring all the time. When the temperature drops below 90°F, 32°C the chocolate is ready to work with. You can put it into moulds, lay it on biscuits or simply lay it out flat on grease proof paper. The easiest way of making chocolate for eating on its own is to lay it thinly in bar sized pieces which can be easily stored then later broken into bite sized slabs. The marble pastry board mentioned earlier is best for this, covered with greaseproof paper, the chocolate will cool quickly this way and temper all the way through to give a glass-like crispness.

Chilli Chocolate Brownies

In my opinion, the most obvious use of chilli chocolate, apart from consumption of the chocolate itself, is the creation of chilli chocolate brownies. I never used to be a chocolate brownie fan; I always found them a bit dry and crumbly.

Even a home-made one with a generous proportion of quality chocolate never really tempted me, though I can consume huge amounts of chocolate on its own. To me, chilli chocolate in a brownie gets the juices flowing and makes it a much more palatable option, a delectable luxury in fact, and served warm with cream or ice cream, even better. Credit for this recipe goes to Holly Jones of the Manna from Devon Cooking School, who shares my chilli chocolate brownie passion.

Ingredients

370g caster sugar

80g cocoa powder

60g plain flour

4 eggs well beaten

250g butter

200g plain chocolate

1 tsp baking powder

¼ habanero chilli

Method

- Preheat your oven to Gas mark 3, 325°F, 170°C.

- Line a 25cm square shallow cake tin with baking parchment or greaseproof paper. Melt the butter slowly in a pan and beat the eggs thoroughly in a bowl. Mix the sugar, cocoa flour and baking powder together in another large bowl. Break up the chocolate into small pieces and stir this into the flour mix along with the chocolate and the melted butter. Add the beaten eggs and stir carefully until the ingredients are all mixed thoroughly. Pour and scrape the mixture into the baking tin and bake for 30-40 minutes. Remove when it is firm and dry on top, but squidgy underneath. You can serve these warm, straight from the tin, or allow them to cool, then slice them and remove them to a cake tin to be eaten later.

- Go easy on the chilli in this recipe, you can spice it up if you like but I think they are best appreciated when mouth-watering, rather than burning.

Hot Chocolate Drink

There are obviously hundreds of recipes for hot chocolate, each of which can be adapted with a bit of chilli, but this is my favourite, and a hugely over indulgent one. I see no reason to compromise where chocolate is concerned. One of the beauties of this recipe is that it demands two types of chocolate, but only 50g of each. As chocolate tends to come in 100g bars there is a lot of welcome leftovers.

This recipe makes two huge mugs or four small ones. You can obviously adjust the quantities pro-rata to suit your needs.

The tricky thing about making a spicy hot chocolate drink with chilli in it is to get the chilli heat to stay in solution, if you use powder on its own then it tends to float to the top unless it is very finely ground and given time to soak, which means some messy and needless pre-preparation.

Another challenge is to get the flavour right, and for this there is only one type of chilli to turn to, and that is the habanero (scotch bonnet) or any of the related *Capsicum chinense* chillies. This is because of their very distinctive fragrant fruity flavour, so different from anything else you might use.

The best method of achieving a good chilli blend is to use fresh chilli.

As I always have a supply of frozen habaneros in the freezer I usually turn to these as they are easy, and don't really add anything to the preparation time. You can cut a piece off, return the rest to the freezer and it will melt as you chop it and you are left with a moist vegetable pulp which you can crush to nothing with the side of your knife. This will mix immediately into your chocolate.

If you have already made your own chilli chocolate then this recipe is where it comes into its own. You can substitute the chocolate for one with chilli in it, and if you only have a very dark chocolate add some sugar to make up the sweetness. Unfortunately you can't really use most of the proprietary chilli chocolates you can buy in the shops as they aren't strong enough to impart any detectable heat to your drink.

Ingredients

500ml milk

100ml double cream

50g milk chocolate

50g strong 70% cocoa chocolate

¼ habanero chilli

Method

- Heat your milk in a pan. Break up all but a tiny piece of your chocolate into pieces in a mug then add a little of the hot milk and the chopped crushed chilli. The chocolate will soon melt and you can mash it to a paste with a spoon to mix in the chilli. Add it to the pan with the cream and gently reheat it all. Stir it with a whisk to blend it and add a little air, I use a small electric cappuccino whisk to froth it up, and be careful not to allow it to boil profusely, just allow it to start bubbling.

- Serve it in big mugs; some of the chocolate you saved can now be grated on top.

Aji and Almond Pralines

These can be an accompaniment to ice cream, or just there to munch on their own; these are a crunchy treat that only take a few minutes to prepare. You can use other hot chillies for this, but the flavour of the aji is quite unique and well suited to this recipe.

Ingredients

100g white sugar

50g flaked almonds

Juice of 1 lime

1 aji limon chilli

Method

- Finely chop the chilli and add it, with the nuts and sugar to a small non-stick pan. Heat it slowly until the sugar melts, stirring it all the time. Keep stirring as the sugar starts to bubble and froth. After a couple of minutes add the lime juice and continue to boil. You are aiming for the sugar to caramelise to a nutty brown colour, at which point you should dollop it, using a tea spoon, onto greaseproof paper. It should soon set with a glass-like appearance, crunchy rather than soft. If it doesn't become crunchy you can scrape it all back into the pan and have another go.

- While it is cooking this is an incredibly hot and dangerous liquid, don't be tempted to taste it.

- The result is some crunchy little sweets, which can be eaten whole, or used to top ice cream. Alternatively whack them with something solid so they break up and stir them into ice cream for a crunchy lemon zing.

Chilli Ice Cream

This is an amazingly quick way of knocking up ice cream that is just as tasty as anything you can buy, even if you don't use the chilli you can use this recipe as a base for other flavours, try chopping in pieces of stem ginger in syrup, or fresh strawberries.

This recipe makes two generous portions, simply multiply the quantities for more.

Ingredients

1 banana

100ml double cream

100ml condensed milk

1 tbsp chilli honey

20g chopped dark chocolate pieces

¼ habanero finely chopped

Method

- Finely chop the habanero piece, if you take one from the freezer you can almost shave off part of it with a knife and return the remainder to the freezer. Mash the habanero and the banana in a bowl. Add the cream, condensed milk and honey. Stir this vigorously until it is almost smooth, there will always be a few lumps of banana, but this helps to give the ice cream a soft feel. After an hour or so in the freezer it should be part-frozen, fold in the chocolate pieces and freeze again for at least another hour. Move it from the freezer to a refrigerator 20 minutes before serving to allow it to soften.

Ginger Chillentines

This recipe replaces dried peel and cherries with ginger, and uses a little habanero or scotch bonnet to add a fruity zap to a classic baked florentine. Eat them on their own or use them as an accompaniment to ice cream. It is one of the most popular things I make; they are completely addictive, and I really can't get enough of them.

This recipe should make around 10 biscuits

Ingredients

25g butter

25g light brown caster sugar

100ml condensed milk

35g plain flour (sieved)

100g chopped crystallised ginger

50g flaked almonds

¼ habanero

100g dark chocolate

Method

- Preheat oven to Gas Mark 4, 180°F, 160°C

- Prepare a baking tray, or trays, by lining them with baking parchment

- Gently heat the butter, condensed milk and sugar in a pan until just bubbling then remove from the heat. Keep stirring it at all times to stop it burning. Add in the flour and almonds then stir until smooth. Finally stir in the ginger. Leave the mixture to cool for a minute or two so that you can pick up a good dollop on a teaspoon and it won't run off too quickly.

- Dollop onto the baking parchment, leave plenty of space between them, the dollops will spread naturally as they cook. Bake in two batches if space doesn't allow for all of them on one tray rather than risking them sticking together. Place them on the top shelf of your oven and cook for approximately 10-12 minutes, but keep an eye on them as they will burn quickly once they are done. If you don't have room on the top shelf for all of them you may wish to cook them in two batches rather than swap them from one shelf to another. Prepare to remove them when the edges start to brown, then do so when the first sign of brown appears on the pointy bits of the middle of the biscuit. Leave them on the baking parchment to cool.

- When the biscuits are cool you can add the chocolate. You will need to heat and temper the chocolate using a bain marie as described in the chilli chocolate recipe. Once the chocolate is ready, 'paint' it onto the flat underside of each chillentine with the back of a spoon. Rest them chocolate side up for a minutes or so until the chocolate has started to set, then, with a fork, make zig-zag patterns on each. The chocolate should be stiff enough at this time to hold the pattern as it sets hard. Stand them somewhere cool, but not in the refrigerator, you don't want them to come into contact with condensation or damp.

Suggested Suppliers

Cool Chile Company – A long-time supplier of Mexican ingredients in the UK and Europe

Cool Chile Co, 1 Enterprise Way, Triangle Business Centre, London NW10 6UG, United Kingdom

Tel: +44 (0)870 902 1145

Web: http://www.coolchile.co.uk/

Email: info@coolchile.co.uk

South Devon Chilli Farm – A long-established supplier of fresh chillies, dried chillies and chilli sauces

South Devon Chilli Farm, Wigford Cross, Loddiswell, Kingsbridge, Devon TQ7 4DX, United Kingdom

Tel: +44(0)1548 550782

Web: http://www.southdevonchillifarm.co.uk/

Edible Ornamentals – A reliable supplier of a wide variety of fresh chillies, especially good for larger quantities

Edible Ornamentals, Cherwood Nursery, Blue Bells, Chawston, Beds MK44 3BL, United Kingdom

Tel: +44 (0)1480 405663

Web: http://www.edibleornamentals.co.uk/

Dowricks Goodlife – Suppliers of home brewing and home preserving accessories, including calcium chloride

Dowricks Goodlife, 3 Barrow Close, Sweetbriar Road Industrial Estate, Norwich, Norfolk NR3 2AT, United Kingdom

Tel: +44(0)1603 418408

Web: https://www.dowricks.com/

Mac's BBQ, Food Smoking Specialists – Suppliers of smoking equipment, including wood sawdust and smoke generators

Unit 3A, Rosevear Rd Industrial Estate, Bugle, Cornwall, UK, PL26 8PJ United Kingdom

Tel: +44(0)1726 851495

Web: http://www.macsbbq.com/

Index